Man and Woman
He Made Them

Other titles by or about Jean Vanier

Tears of Silence
Community and Growth
The Broken Body
Treasures of the Heart (Daily Readings with Jean Vanier)
Jean Vanier and l'Arche (by Kathryn Spink)

Man and Woman He Made Them

JEAN VANIER

Foreword by Henri J. M. Nouwen

DARTON · LONGMAN + TODD

First published in Great Britain in 1985 by
Darton, Longman and Todd Ltd
1 Spencer Court
140–142 Wandsworth High Street
London SW18 4JJ

Reprinted 1985, 1986, 1987, 1989, 1990, 1992, 1994 and 1997

Originally published in French by Editions Fleurus and Editions
Bellarmin in 1984 under the title *Homme et Femme Il les Fit*

British Library Cataloguing in Publication Data

Vanier, Jean
    Man and woman he made them.
    1. Interpersonal relations—Religious aspects—
    Christianity   2. Men   3. Women
    I. Title
    261.8′35   BT702

    ISBN 0–232–51642–1

Phototypeset by Intype, London
Printed and bound in Great Britain by
Page Bros, Norwich

Contents

Contents

Foreword

Perhaps the best way to introduce Jean Vanier to you is to tell you how Jean entered into my life. This should help explain the way this book is written.

One day, when I was living in New Haven, Connecticut, a woman named Jan Risse came to my home and said: 'I come to bring you greetings from Jean Vanier.' I had heard about Jean and his l'Arche Communities for people who are mentally handicapped, but had never met him. As on other occasions I expected this greeting to be followed by a request to give a lecture, write an article, offer a retreat. So I said: 'Thank you . . . and what can I do for you?' Jan Risse smiled and said: 'Nothing. Jean just wants you to know that he is thinking of you and praying for you, and hopes that maybe one day or one year you both will meet.' Jan stayed for a few days, made a wonderful meal for me in my own house with candles, flowers, and plates I didn't even know I had. She came to one of my lectures and offered her help in all sorts of small ways. She indeed became my host! When she left she said again: 'Just know that Jean is thinking about you and praying for you.'

Two years later, Jean called me from Chicago and invited me to make a silent retreat at Pentecost with him. We exchanged a few words, but mostly were together in prayer. Nothing very special or interesting. But during that quiet Pentecost, a friendship began to grow. I went to visit him at the l'Arche Community in Trosly, France, first for a few weeks and later for a few months. Now I am wondering if that 'useless' visit by Jan Risse wasn't God's gentle way of calling me into a direction I never had dreamt of going.

I am telling you this simple story because the Jean Vanier of my story is the same Jean Vanier who is beside you on every page of this book. He does not push you, argue with you, or try to get you on his side. He simply speaks to you in a very quiet, conversational tone, introduces you to some of the people he has lived with for many years, tells some stories and lets you think for yourself. At first you might not notice it, but gradually you will come to realize that Jean's presence brings you in touch with a place inside yourself that few people have reached. It is the vulnerable but also very creative place where God's love resides.

As you read the reflections in this book you will find yourself saying: 'yes . . . yes . . . this is true . . . I know it . . . but maybe it was too simple a truth for me to grasp.' Living as you do in a world in which complexity is rewarded more than simplicity, Jean's heartfelt words about men and women and their relationships to each other will touch you by their purity and transparency.

I am convinced that this is the most important book that Jean Vanier has written. He draws upon twenty years of experience of living with mentally handicapped people and their assistants, and offers this experience as a source of learning to all who are willing to raise basic questions about the hard but joyful task of living together as human beings. He speaks from a deep and vibrant faith in the all-embracing love of God, and also gives many practical suggestions for daily use. This is a book about intimacy and sexuality, about being distant and getting close, about unity and diversity, about servanthood and authority, about growth and maturity, about work and love, in short, about life.

When I read this book I feel Jean taking me by the arm, walking with me from house to house, inviting me to listen, look, learn, and join in the life there. 'These wounded men and women,' he seems to say, 'are your teachers. They do not hide anything, they tell you things about agony and ecstasy that no book ever will. They are God's messengers revealing to you what you most desperately want to know: the mystery of love.'

The awesome beauty of this book is that it gives a voice to those who are least respected and honoured in our society – the mentally handicapped – and allows them to respond to our most personal desire: to find a fruitful home. Men and women who are often not able to develop sexual relationships teach us about true intimacy. Men and women who cannot bear children or live outwardly productive lives teach us about true fruitfulness.

Men and women who can only dance or sing with great difficulty teach us what it means to celebrate life. Men and women who by many are not considered fully human teach us what being human is all about.

Here lies Jean Vanier's great gift. He listens to those who are least listened to and speaks words that they cannot speak, but which hold a wisdom born of their wounded existence. What finally emerges from this human brokenness is the face of a God whose love is without limitation, a God who wants to be so intimately connected with us that we can bear with our own and others' limitations and live in peace. Jean Vanier is more than a good observer who helps us see the basic human questions which arise out of life with people who are mentally handicapped. He is a pastor who gently and patiently points to the presence of God where we least expect it.

The most moving and healing news of this book is that the discovery of the absolute love of God allows us to accept the relative and imperfect love of people. Those with mental handicaps, who are so clearly dependent on relative signs of love and acceptance, can be so joyous and radiant since somehow they know that beyond the wounds and needs of others there is an embrace without conditions or restraint. Thus they teach us to see the limited expressions of human affection as refractions of the unlimited love of God.

It is clear that not everyone who lives with mentally handicapped people sees what Jean Vanier sees. Jean is not a social worker who happens to be a Christian. He is first and foremost a man of God. He is always and everywhere searching for God, wherever and with whomever he is. His whole life has been in the service of this search, as a young man in the navy, as a student in France, as a professor in Canada. He finally found God among people with mental handicaps, with whom he started to live in France. With them, he has created homes all over the world. Indeed he found God, but his search continues, for God is far greater than his heart and mind. The God whom Jean has found searches for himself deeper and deeper in the hearts of wounded people.

When you finish reading this book, with its anecdotes, stories, and countless vignettes of wisdom, you will have received more than just new insights into human intimacy and fruitfulness. You will come to a new and moving vision of God, who loved us‐so much that he came to dwell among us and make a true home here with us. We are all handicapped, we all search for a home, we all desire to live intimate and fruitful lives. God comes to us with open hands, calling out again and again: 'Come to me, all you who are over-burdened, and I will give you rest.'

When Jan Risse came to visit me I did not think much about it. But a few years later my life had been opened up to a new horizon. When you read this book you might at first consider it innocent, lovely maybe, but somewhat obvious. But I can assure you, if you let Jean Vanier come close to you and listen carefully to what he has to say, you might soon find yourself a different person.

HENRI J. M. NOUWEN

In this book I speak about Eric. He died at l'Arche at the very time I was giving the French manuscript to the publisher. We loved Eric very much in the community. I lived with him for a year. He taught me so much. Eric was a very limited person, fragile, blind, deaf and with a severe mental handicap. But he knew how to awaken hearts and lead us towards the light. We lived a covenant together.

With him, part of the community is now in Heaven and a part of Heaven is now present in the community.

I dedicate this book to him. May he help us live, work and struggle, so that the poorest and the weakest be honoured and find their place in the Church and in the world.

I am grateful to friends with whom I shared the first manuscript of this book. Their criticism helped me to make my thoughts more clear and precise. I give thanks in a special way to Claire de Miribel, and to Gilles and Dominique Lecardinal. If this book has been published it is largely thanks to them. We worked on it together. I could not have done it without their competent and supportive help. Special thanks also to Elizabeth Buckley who translated the book into English, and to Chris Sadler who reviewed the text with clarity and wisdom.

Introduction

This book is a witness to the twenty years I have spent in
l'Arche, where I have lived day by day with people who have a
mental handicap.

My first meeting with someone having a mental handicap was
not planned. I entered the Navy at the age of thirteen, during
the war in 1942. My education was geared to efficiency. Then,
inspired by the Gospel of Jesus and by the call to work for peace,
I resigned my commission. My last ship was the aircraft carrier,
the *Magnificent*, of the Royal Canadian Navy. In 1950, I went to
France to live in a Christian community founded by Father
Thomas Philippe near Paris. There we lived simply, learning to
pray and to work with our hands. We also studied philosophy
and theology, which for me led to a doctorate in Philosophy on
the ethics of Aristotle. After receiving my degree, I began to
teach in St Michael's College at the University of Toronto.

So, nothing had prepared me for my encounter with rejected
people when I went back to visit Father Thomas at Trosly-
Breuil in 1963. He was then the chaplain for the Val Fleuri, a
residence for thirty men with mental handicaps.

I was surprised and bewildered by the meeting. These men
were so different from my students in Toronto! The latter were
impressed, more or less, by what I could give them from my
head so that they could pass their exams; but they were not
really interested in me as a person. Those whom I met at Trosly
were totally uninterested in the contents of my head, but very
interested in my person. 'What's your name?' 'What do you do?'
'When will you come back to see us?' They were crying out for a
relationship. Their whole bodies, indeed their whole being, had
obviously been deprived of friendship and affection. Their cry
for friendship touched me and awoke something deep inside me.

These men who were mentally handicapped were so simple

1

and so true in their cry. The values of the heart were so alive in them. Since I left the Navy, these values had become important in my life as a disciple of Jesus. However, in some respects, my heart was still entrenched behind barriers of efficiency, reason, and even my own will. These wounded and thirsty hearts were like a call which echoed in my own heart.

As I have said in *The Challenge of l'Arche*,[1] where I tell the story in detail, I felt, through these men and through Father Thomas, a call from God to share my own life with people who had a mental handicap. When I welcomed Raphael and Philippe from the asylum in which they had been shut up, into the old, little house which I had procured in the village of Trosly-Breuil, I knew that I had taken an irreversible step. It all happened so simply. I was a little naive. I did not have any big plans. I just took a leap in the dark, or rather I let myself be drawn into bonds of love which – this I more or less realized – would tie me for life. I was · aware of taking a risk. But, at the same time, I sensed in all this a call or an invitation from God, and I was confident. It was as if God was saying to me: 'Don't be afraid; I am with you.'

In welcoming and listening to Raphael and Philippe, and so many others who had been put aside, I let myself be carried into an unknown world. I discovered the depths of their sufferings, the cry within them for authentic relationships, as well as the joy of living together.

When I started to live with men and women who were more or less disfigured, I wanted to give them a human face. In so doing, I discovered that it was they who gave a human face to me. They opened me to the discovery of my own humanity. They drew me, almost in spite of myself, into the heart of community life and into the heart of the Beatitudes and the Gospels. They helped me discover the meaning of a covenant with another and how it is founded on a covenant with God. I also discovered that all forgiveness and all celebration – the most essential elements of community life – are founded on these covenants. My book, *Community and Growth*,[2] is an account of all they have taught me in this domain.

1. 1981. For the beginnings of l'Arche one can also read the excellent book by Bill Clarke, s.j., *Enough Room for Joy*, 1974.
2. 1979. This book explains the basic principles of community life.

2

Introduction

Obviously, in living with men having a mental handicap, one is confronted with numerous problems. One is faced with different kinds of crises and violence which spring from very wounded and anguished hearts. I had everything to learn. The difficulties increased when, after the departure of nearly all its staff, I was asked to take responsibility for the Val Fleuri where Father Thomas was chaplain. There was so much anguish in that house that I sometimes felt completely overwhelmed. There were men drawn to homosexuality and masturbation, even to the point of exhibitionism. One man even walked through the village totally naked. I tried to understand and help them. I made rules. I did the best I could in new and complex circumstances.

It became evident to me during these difficult years that there is a link between the anguished, wounded heart, the cry of violence, and disturbed sexuality. It was necessary, first of all, to make the homes of l'Arche and the Val places where suffering hearts could find peace. Gradually, we were able to make them places of life, tenderness and friendship, indeed truly a 'home'. As the violence began to diminish, so did many manifestations of uncontrolled sexuality. The men began to take on a more human face.

I had begun the first home of l'Arche with men. The Val Fleuri was also only for men. In 1969, we opened the first home for women at Cuise la Motte, about three miles from Trosly. Gradually the workshops began to integrate both men and women and new homes were started, some solely for men or for women, others mixed. Now, in 1984, in the region of Trosly and Compiègne, there are more than twenty such homes, not to mention the apartments and houses of welcome for visitors.

Since the creation of the first home in 1964 until today, twenty years later, when there are over seventy l'Arche communities throughout the world (representing nearly 200 homes), many questions concerning sexuality have arisen. Naturally men and women have been attracted to one another. Some couples have been formed. There have also been instances of men being attracted to children and others to exhibitionism. There have been acts of homosexuality and masturbation. All of this obviously poses questions for the teams of assistants. The most important question is how to understand the origins and

3

meaning of these different behaviours, and how to develop comprehensive attitudes which are both true and educative.

At the beginning of l'Arche, and especially of the Val, when there was a lot of violence, all our energies had to be directed to the creation of a harmonious environment where each person could find inner peace. It necessitated passing through a stage of authority and organization, creating well-defined structures, giving security so that a certain peace and a new dynamism could emerge. Only then were we able to concentrate on listening to the needs of each one, building a project with and for him, requiring that we give a greater space for liberty for each one. L'Arche became more personalized, each home more like a small family.

I was a little lost, as I faced all the problems. The human being is so complex, so rich in possibilities for growth, yet so vulnerable and fragile, so quick to lose confidence in self and in others. I had so much to learn, and I believe I learned more through my mistakes and failures than through the successes! In questions pertaining to life, there is no real success, only growth. While I tried to listen to the needs and the crises of each one, my vision of the human being, of his or her needs and growth, was inspired by my Christian faith and by my own education. I saw that this vision brought a certain well-being and inner liberty to others.

THE CONCEPT OF 'NORMALIZATION'

In 1964 there were few centres for adults with a mental handicap. Since then, many have come into existence. More and more, people are being deinstitutionalized. For example, in the United States the number of people in institutions has been reduced from 173,000 in 1973 to 130,000 in 1979.[3] By 1980, in the state of New York, 700 group homes were established in residential areas of towns and cities.

A kind of revolution had begun, especially in the 1970s. People began to discover that those with a mental handicap had aston-

---

3. *From the 60's to the 80's: an International Assessment of Attitudes and Services for the Developmentally Disabled.* Young Adults Institute and Workshop, Inc. (New York, 1982), p. 16.

ishing potential for growth, that many who had been stigmatized were able to work and live happily like everyone else.

Thus was born in the rich countries, especially in Scandinavia, the principles called 'normalization' for those with a mental handicap. According to these principles, those people with a handicap must live like everyone else; at any price, segregation must be avoided. Treat someone like a fool and that person becomes a fool. To fear someone is to instil in that person a fear of himself or herself and fear of others. Similarly, a person who is treated as 'normal', will become 'normal'.

I discovered this for myself, as I lived with men and women who had been locked up in asylums. The way you look at people can transform them.

But 'normalization' raises some questions, especially concerning relations between men and women with mental handicaps. Relationships are made in the residences, the workshops or institutions where both sexes are present. What are the rights of those with a mental handicap in relation to marriage and sexual relationships? What kind of intervention should be made when a man and a woman are attracted to each other? Should limits to their affectionate encounter be imposed?

Often, in the past, parents tended to ignore these questions. People with a mental handicap were considered 'asexual'. At the other extreme, they were seen as sexually disturbed and dangerous, especially in relation to children; that is why so many were locked up in big institutions, deprived of their freedom.

The 'normalization' movement wants to 'normalize' all aspects of life, including the sexual life, of those with a mental handicap. In many of the rich countries an active sexual life is encouraged. N. E. Banks-Mikkelson, director of services for those with mental handicaps in Denmark, writes:

> The mentally retarded adult must be treated as an adult, and be accepted with an adult's characteristics, for instance, be accepted also as a sexually developed adult. The latter problem is hedged, as a rule, with many rooted prejudices that are apt to be intensified in the case of handicapped people's sexual life. Handicapped persons will generally be normally developed in this respect and must be entitled to a natural sex-life.[4]

4. Op. cit., 'The Principle of Normalization', p. ix.

Normalization insists, then, on the importance of sexual relations for the human development of a man or a woman with a mental handicap. It is necessary, therefore, to instruct and help them to live and to develop their sexuality fully because they have a right to sexual pleasure.

IMPLICATIONS OF THE 'NORMALIZATION' OF SEXUAL RELATIONS

We are touching here a difficult question. The desire to 'normalize', to help someone with a mental handicap make choices and find personal autonomy, seems good. What is possible in this area? How should we respond to these theories of normalization of sexuality and the right of each human being to sexual pleasure?

Some educators and psychologists say excessive things regarding this. They themselves wish to 'be free' and intend to help others toward sexual liberation. They speak of the right to sexual pleasure, but very little of the right to relationships. It is as if genital sexuality was entirely cut off from the person and from life.

There are others – and I believe they are the majority – who are searching and feeling their way. Perhaps they are reacting against a traditional view of sexuality. But they also recognize the value of a permanent relationship between a man and a woman; they hear the cry for intimacy and friendship. They tend to favour and even encourage their living together as couples in the residences where this is possible. At the same time, they feel anxiety and concern. They don't like to forbid, because they themselves don't like to be forbidden. Nevertheless, they are upset and confused when acts of genital sexuality take place in public. They want people to be autonomous and free, but they systematically administer the Pill, or even force people to be sterilized. Most of them have misgivings, sensing that there are contradictions in their attitudes; they know that often they are giving a double message.

At l'Arche, from the beginning, I took a clear position, even if it was a bit simplistic: freedom in sexual relations was not allowed, but we acknowledged the possibility that some people

6

might be guided towards a greater autonomy and, eventually, towards human love in the bonds of marriage.

REFLECTING ON OUR VISION AT L'ARCHE

Faced with different and sometimes contradictory theories concerning the emotional and sexual life of those with a mental handicap, we at l'Arche felt the need to deepen our own vision.

We were no longer able to remain on the level of intuitions or with the passive acceptance of a Christian ethic. We had to understand and to respond positively, with wisdom and not just by prohibitions, to different situations in which the sexual urge is expressed: homosexuality, masturbation, sexual obsessions, violence of different kinds, formation of couples which do not appear to lead either one to growth. Above all, we needed to know how to help the men and women for whom we were responsible in their quest for relationship and in all their suffering. We had to deepen our intellectual, psychological, and human vision of the emotional and sexual life.

We had to explore what might be considered an ethic for men and women with a mental handicap, for those who cannot be fully autonomous. In order to live, they have need to be supported and 'accompanied' in this, as in other areas of their lives. Besides, there are laws for growth in all humans, and in order to live together in society we must always accept certain regulations. On the other hand, purely negative prohibitions and repressive attitudes cannot be factors for growth. Traditional ethics presupposes that one understands the law and the rules, that one has a certain strength of will in order to temper sexual urges and avoid the risk of hurting oneself and others. But someone with a mental handicap has deficiencies on the rational and volitional levels, even though they often have a deep intuition of what is good, true and right. Yet usually, if they are not in a supportive milieu, they have neither the will nor the mastery of self necessary to avoid being dominated by these impulses and overpowering drives and by the crises to which they lead. They rarely have sufficient inner autonomy and freedom to direct their lives alone. They are often impressionable and dependent on their surroundings.

In order to help someone with a mental handicap who has real sexual difficulties, it is not enough to impose prohibitions or to rely simply on dialogue. We must help the person to find new energies, a deeper freedom, other centres of attraction and interest. We must discover how to help people, not simply to control their sexual compulsions, but to pacify their genital sexuality at its roots. In other words, we must discover the deep meaning and the richness of that sexuality, but also, its limits and its relativity.

This book is the fruit of these quests and tensions. It springs from our difficulties, our confusions, our search and, above all, from being close to the suffering of those with mental handicaps. It is an attempt to understand the basis and the deep meaning of sexuality: what is it we seek in a sexual relationship, and what are the most fundamental needs of a human being?

But, more important than asking philosophical questions is the necessity of responding to concrete situations: What can we do when a man or a woman who is very deficient masturbates, in private or in public? What can we do when a man and a woman, both with deficiencies, are attracted to each other and exchange gestures of affection and tenderness? Can they marry? Will they be able to have children? What can we do when a man with a mental handicap is attracted sexually by children? What can we do with that young woman, of whom I heard, who periodically escapes from the psychiatric hospital and, each time, conceives a child? Should she be sterilized . . .? And what about abortion?

When we live with those who have profound emotional needs, there are so many situations that can arise! So many cries, so much suffering.

Each day I discover more and more how human sexuality is a reality which is, at the same time, both precious and painful. Each human being is incomplete; our bodies are incomplete: man has need of the woman, woman has need of the man. The fact of being a man or a woman influences the biological, psychic, moral and spiritual realities of each one. And each is drawn towards the other, each is made for the other. Humanity continues to exist thanks to that complementarity. There would be no fecundity, no fruitfulness, without the union of the two. But man is able to oppress the woman, debase her, ridicule her, treat her as an object. If he is not unified within himself, if his sexuality is not well integrated in his being and his emotional life, man will tend to denigrate and exploit woman. Instead of seeing her as a companion, his beloved, a person called to grow, he will want to conquer her and possess her for himself. Thus, he is incapable of relationship. And the woman knows how to take her secret revenge on the man. There is therefore, nothing more important than to help the man and the woman to integrate their sexuality in and through an authentic love, so that it may open them to a true relationship and a profound communion.

When a man and a woman truly love each other, whether it be through the tenderness and communion of marriage or in celibacy and community life, there is nothing more beautiful. It is the gift of God to humanity. Their love is the root of the 'body' which is the community. It is the power of unity which will inspire all other unities; it is the power of healing which will inspire all other healings. It is fruitful with a spiritual fruitfulness.

This book is not a treatise on the sexuality of those with a mental handicap. It does not seek to give precise solutions to all those questions, always complex, which we will encounter. Those who want clear answers to particular problems will certainly be disappointed. The complexity of human reality and the depth of certain wounds are such that there are no clear or easy solutions. This book seeks to share the sufferings and the quest of those with a mental handicap whom I have known and accompanied. It is, in part, a reflection on the source of these sufferings and on the profound meaning of human affection and sexuality. It is, also, an attempt on my part to show what principles and directions have guided us in our choice of attitudes when faced with concrete situations. Beyond these considerations, this book is an invitation to begin to make your own reflections.

If you share the global vision which this book presents, you may be able, together with a team and perhaps also with the person concerned, to find an answer yourself to the questions you ask. Above all, we must, within a network of friendship, accompany people with their sufferings and their needs, as they struggle towards greater maturity of their affectivity, so that eventually they can attain an interior liberty and move to a greater communion with others – so that they, in their turn, will be better able to love and serve.

MY CHRISTIAN FAITH

This book is written from the daily experience of our life in Trosly and the different communities of l'Arche, but also in the context of my own Christian experience, my trust in Jesus and in the Good News which he brought. Sexuality should never be separated from love; if it is, it becomes false, manipulative, and it fragments the person. The Good News of Jesus is a reality of love. It would be inadequate for me to look at sexual questions outside the Christian perspective of this reality. Certainly, I could have addressed parents and professionals without making explicit my faith in the Gospel message and the inspiration it gives me. The values which we discover in this area of the emotional and sexual life are, I believe, verifiable in everyday experience. But I was afraid of thus toning down reality, perhaps even distorting my thought. I believe it is more pertinent and truthful to explain openly my experience without hiding the underlying inspiration.

That is why this book, without excluding the professionals and parents who do not have faith in Jesus, is addressed above all to Christian readers. My experience has shown me that there is no rupture between the message of the Gospel and psychology. In fact, the more I deepen the essence of my faith in that love which springs from the heart of God, the more it helps me to understand the sufferings, the deep call, the crying out of the human being. And, the closer I come to people in their humanity, listening to them and sensing their needs, the more I am confirmed in my faith in Jesus and the essence of his teaching.

This book is to thank God for having created us man and woman. Each one, alone, is fragile and incomplete, but through an authentic love which is communion and gift, a unity is given which draws us from our loneliness and makes us enter the heart of a God who is Father, Son, and Holy Spirit.

1

The Wounded Heart

THE DISILLUSIONMENT OF PARENTS

A person with a mental handicap has deep wounds in his or her heart and affections. These wounds can seriously affect the sexuality of the person, which may then become quite disturbed. A handicap is often very visible. It is written on the face, the legs and the hands. It is apparent in the person's speech or lack of speech, in the inability to reason, to plan and to face the future. The wounded heart, on the other hand, is hidden, revealing itself through fear, lack of confidence, depression, violence, fantasies and withdrawal from reality. Above all, it is manifested by a broken image of self, a profound guilt and a refusal of life.

The person with a mental handicap is a disappointment to the parents who expected a beautiful, healthy child, looking like them, a child in whom they had placed much hope. At the time of birth, or after an illness or accident, they saw the handicap in the face and body of their child. Doctors confirmed their fears, perhaps brutally: 'Your child is severely handicapped. We can do nothing. Put him away and plan to have another as soon as possible.' In an instant, their hearts were crushed, their hopes shattered; and anger was born. 'Why has this happened to us? What have we done to deserve this?' Then, because it is necessary to blame someone, comes the terrible question: 'Whose fault is this?' In the Gospel (John 9:2) the apostles ask the question about the man born blind: 'Master, who has sinned, this man or his parents?' They are asking: 'Who is guilty?' Is the child with a handicap a punishment from God? And if so, how can the fault be expiated?

More and more I am touched by the sufferings and difficulties of parents. At l'Arche, we have our days off, our holidays, our times of renewal and spiritual refreshment. We have chosen to live with handicapped people. Parents have no days off, little support and no chance to refresh their spirits. They did not choose their child to be 'like that'. For them, it is a tragedy, a personal humiliation, and constant suffering. We at l'Arche are often admired for our 'dedication'; parents, on the other hand, are often pitied or looked down upon. A whole school of psychological thought even blames them, especially if the child is psychotic. There are many heroic parents who live long days and often long nights with terribly disturbed children. There are no schools, centres or special workshops near their homes. They do not have competent or understanding psychologists and doctors to encourage and support them. Often shunned by neighbours, friends, and even family and church, they find themselves terribly alone, utterly abandoned. Believing they are punished by God, they close in on themselves in isolation and anguish.

THE SUFFERING OF THE CHILD

All these sufferings deeply affect the child. It is a terrible thing for a child to feel it has let its parents down and is the cause of their pain and their tears. The wounded hearts of parents wound the heart of the child. A healthy child senses itself as the cause of joy and the centre of delighted attention, one whom everyone wants to touch, to hug and to hold. The child senses the pride and joy of its parents as each new skill is gradually developed and acquired. Between the baby and its parents, there is a life-giving dialogue which stimulates, calls forth, encourages and supports. The tiniest baby senses whether or not it is truly precious to parents, loved by them in a unique way.

Sometimes I am asked: 'Is a child or an adult who has a severe mental handicap aware of his or her condition? Do they suffer from this?' For the most part, I don't know. But this I do know: the tiniest infant senses if it is loved and wanted, or not. Similarly, people with a mental handicap, even a severe one, sense immediately whether they are loved and valued by the way they are looked at, spoken to and welcomed.

A new-born child is extremely fragile and vulnerable. Unable to do anything alone, he or she must be fed, washed and held. There is only one recourse, which is to cry. If the baby feels loved and valued, there is a feeling of security and safety; the baby is able to live, to be at ease and ,to enter with confidence into relationships with others and with the reality of the world. However, the life of a baby who does not feel loved and valued is in danger; other people and the surroundings become threatening. Then, the baby enters into the world of fear and insecurity, where one instinctively hardens oneself in order to protect oneself and thus to survive. The child suffers terribly; he or she lives in anguish.

A child also lives in anguish and experiences a form of interior death if its mother is too possessive and has invested herself too exclusively in him or her. Somehow she communicates the fear of separation, and through this can smother life. Every child is called to leave its parents. Therefore, children must learn early in life to cope with separation and frustration. This is as necessary for their growth as it is to be loved and valued. True love does not imprison; it liberates. A mother cannot be occupied totally with her child; she has a husband also, and she has her own needs. The child must learn the frustrations of separation in order to discover the joys of reunion with parents and to put his or her confidence in the bonds which unite them all together.

Few people seem to understand the depth of the anguish of a tiny child who is not loved or who is 'badly' loved. Fortunately, scientific research, focusing on the newborn infant, is discovering today what mothers have always known: that the relationship between the mother and child is profoundly sacred and precious, a source of life for them both.

Today, human science has ascertained, in part, that a newborn infant cannot only see and hear (though in a very limited way), but can even recognize the smell of its mother. We know that an intense dialogue, harmony, relationship already exist between the baby and the mother – even before the child is born. If that relationship is defective, if the little one does not sense its mother's love – which not only rejoices in her baby's beauty and uniqueness, but also in its potential for growth, for autonomy and eventual separation from her – then the baby feels lost and enters into anguish. It experiences either an inner emptiness or an inner suffocation.

ANGUISH

Anguish is a terrible reality, the greatest of human sufferings. This is why it is used in torture. When the victim suffers total anguish, there is a sense of terrible confusion, of being utterly lost. Then he or she will be unable to keep any secret.

Anguish first reveals itself in the region of the solar plexus, the seat of the emotions, and then spreads throughout the whole body. Inner balance is broken, and the person becomes agitated, confused, unable to reason or to judge. The normal digestive and sleep cycles are destroyed, with a tendency to eat and sleep too much or not at all.

This state of anguish is so terrible that it cannot be tolerated for long. In order to survive and escape the pain, the child protects itself by creating defences, in particular by cutting itself off from the deep feelings of the heart and hiding in a world of dreams. When the heart of a person is solidly barricaded in this way, there is psychosis. If the barriers are less solid, there is instability, sometimes deep depression, agitation, apathy or aggression.

In the case of adolescents or adults, the defences may take on different forms. Some escape into hyperactivity, a burning desire to succeed, to win, to dominate; others search for compensation in alcohol, drugs, sexual encounters, a continual search for distraction and pleasure. Still others sink into depression, mental illnesses, or delinquency.

When I see Evelyn banging her head against the floor, when I hear Robert in the middle of the night begging someone to cut off his genitals, when I see Luke aimlessly running round and round, when I see the closed, tense face of George, I know in each there is a profound agony and an unbearable interior restlessness.

A baby who has a mental handicap, sensing that it is not wanted, will harden its heart and body and, to protect itself, will withdraw from reality. There is thus a sort of inner death: life no longer evolves. Agitation prevents development. Certain aspects of the psychic being become blocked. The brain, language and even physical development are all affected. Thus begins the fragmentation of the being.

I remember John Mark seated next to me in the chapel, whispering over and over: 'I have the devil in me. I have evil in me.' The story of John Mark is a story of rejection. Born in a psychiatric hospital, abandoned by his mother, he was adopted, but this did not work out. He then went from one foster family to another. After a time, he was placed in a small institution and then sent to a psychiatric hospital because he had shown signs of violence. At the age of 27, he came to l'Arche. Never in his life had he had a lasting and unique relationship with an adult. Moved from one place to another, he had never heard anyone say to him, 'You are my beloved son and you are my joy. Between us is an indestructible bond. No matter what you do, you will always be my child.' John Mark was without any roots.

If one has never been loved, how can one believe oneself to be lovable? And if one is not lovable, then it must be because one is evil. The logic of love is relentless. Because no one ever had confidence in him, because no one had ever formed a bond with him, John Mark was not able to have confidence in himself. He had a negative image of himself. Perhaps John Mark is an extreme example, but how many handicapped people suffer from the image they have been given of themselves?

There is Yvette, who was welcomed into one of our communities and who had been considered a crazy idiot since her early childhood. She is imprisoned in that image and continually tries to live up to it.

I remember Michael who, when he won a gold medal in the Special Olympics, wept and cried out: 'Do you think that now my mother will believe I am good for something?'

There is Georgette who, when asked if she would like to be married some day, replied: 'I will never marry because my mother told me that if I married I might have a child like me.'

I am always struck by the way each is the reflection of how he or she is seen by others. Gloria, who lives in a l'Arche community in a Latin-American slum, acts so differently now compared to the time when she was with her family who scorned her. At home, family and neighbours looked on her as the 'village idiot'. In our home, where she is treated with hope, respect and understanding, she is adjusting more and more; her personality is becoming more structured despite her crises. Girls like her lie in wait to see if others look at them in fear, judgement, scorn, and superiority, or with understanding, kindness and joy in her presence. The eyes are the mirror where each of us discovers who we are. 'Who am I for you?' Gloria is so much who we see her to be. And she is capable of interpreting the tiniest nuance: 'You love me because I gave you a gift? You love me because I am making progress? You love me because through me you found a meaning to your life?' Or, rather, 'You love me for me, because my life means something?'

These are only a few examples. I could give hundreds of others, showing the deep suffering of mentally handicapped people, and how the negative, broken image they have of themselves comes from the image others have of them. Dr Dolto, a child psychiatrist, at a session for special educators in France, once explained how the psychotic child identifies himself with human excrement. Always feeling rejection, always perceiving himself as bad, he identifies himself with what is rejected as waste and which smells bad.

I am always impressed by the love people with a mental handicap have for their parents, even when there are no grounds for such love, even when they have been mistreated and abandoned. People who have a mental handicap always hope for the happy and loving reunion with their parents, even when their waiting and their hope are so often disappointed and dashed to the ground. I have never heard one of them criticize or judge his or her parents. The tragedy is rather that they condemn themselves as if they deserved their parents' rejection. They feel and develop a profound sense of guilt because they feel it is they who are bad and evil.

Let me tell you about Betty. She had lived with an impossible mother, a 'bad' mother. She has endured so much that now she is unable to live with a woman assistant without persecuting her, without avenging herself. But, is it truly revenge? Is it not rather a cry: 'You see, you will never be able to love me; I am too bad.' Thus, she relives the conflict with her mother.

One of the difficulties of the child, but also found between engaged couples or husband and wife, is to idealize the parent (or the other), to turn them into idols. They become as gods who ought to fulfil every need. When this doesn't happen, then the child either feels it is its own fault or rejects the one who has not lived up to its expectations. It is so difficult in any relationship to accept the loved one as a fallible person who also has needs, and to avoid projecting one's own needs on to the other.

I remember a meeting at l'Arche to discuss a man who had been severely rejected by his family and who was quite disturbed. Dr Franko, then the psychiatrist of our community, said of him: 'He feels guilty for existing.' So many of the men and women we welcome into l'Arche have been considered to be difficult and unbearable by their families (and often they have been). They have been treated only in negative terms, as idiots, disabled, deficient. It is not surprising they feel guilty, responsible for the tears and anguish of their parents. It is not surprising that they have cut themselves off from their hearts; they have suffered too much. They cannot bear the pain any more.

This deep wound of the heart is the source of their bizarre behaviour, whether aggressive or depressive. Not having been recognized as true human beings, capable of growth, they are unable even to begin forming a true relationship with another. Having always been considered by others as an object, they will consider others as objects; they cannot imagine that they are capable of giving life and happiness to another. In order to live they must make the transition from a negative self-image to a positive image, from a feeling of being without value to a feeling of being valued. Who will help them make this transition?

This inner fragmentation is not restricted to people who have a mental handicap. It is found in all unwanted children, children who feel they are a burden. These, too, must protect themselves from unbearable pain. I remember a prisoner, condemned for kidnapping a child, telling me that his mother had told him when he was eight years old: 'If the contraceptives had worked, you would not be here today.'

Symptoms of depression are often found, not only in such children, but also in people who are scorned because of their race, their poverty, or their inabilities.

These same wounds are found also, though to a lesser degree, in the hearts of all children. This becomes clearer and clearer to me each day. Every child, some day or other, has felt more or less let down by its parents, has felt unloved, unappreciated. Parents go through periods of depression; they are taken up by their own problems and needs and do not give adequate attention to caring for their child. And the heart of a child is so vulnerable and sensitive! These wounds which remain in the unconscious produce difficulties in future relationships, and even in the use of one's sexuality. They accentuate a separation between genital sexuality and the heart, between the search for sexual pleasure for self and the search for an authentic and deep relationship with another who is seen as a unique person having his or her own needs and freedom.

However, it seems evident – to anyone who knows all kinds of families, united or divided, all kinds of parents, over-protective or unloving or, on the other hand, very present and loving – that a wounded heart is not produced in a child only by the attitudes of parents. Even the most marvellous parents can never fulfil every hope and need in the child. They are able to love their child, but they are not able to ensure that the child's heart will itself be loving. Certainly, in a child, there is great innocence and beauty but, regardless of all the qualities of its parents, there are also all kinds of fear, fragility and egotism. In the heart of a child there is always a void which can be filled only by an infinite love. This is the glory and the tragedy of humankind. St Augustine's words, 'My heart is restless until it rests in God', applies to each and every human being. The wounded heart of every child, with its selfishness and fear, comes from an awareness of this emptiness deep within our being which we desperately try to fill. This void is an anguish but, if the child has even a minimum of confidence, it can become a driving force towards a search for truth.

Christian doctrine on the wounded heart, or original sin, appears to me the one reality which is easily verified. It would be an error to believe that if there were no oppressive parents, if there was no oppressive society, then we would have only beautiful children, loving, happy, integrated within themselves. No, in the heart of each of us, there is division, there is fear, there is fragility; there is a defence system which protects our vulnerability, there is flight from pain, there is evil and there is darkness. However, the child who has relationships which help and truly support, will find hope and trust to go forward in the search for true fulfilment.

HEALING THE HEART: A REDEEMING LOVE

Eric was sixteen years old when we welcomed him to l'Arche some years ago. He had been placed in a hospital at the age of four; he was blind, deaf, severely brain-damaged and his heart terribly wounded by being abandoned by his family.

In the hospital there were doctors and nurses who cared for him, but none were able to answer the deep cries of his heart. They were not there to establish lasting and loving relationships with him. Hospitals are not homes but places for treatment.

The body of a child who senses it is loved and secure is relaxed. A child who feels abandoned and alone becomes rigid and tense, so as not to suffer too much anguish. Thus it was with Eric who protected himself against an environment which he perceived as hostile, because it was incapable of responding to his cry and his enormous need for tenderness. The rigidity of Eric's heart had become a rigidity of his whole body. His muscles were like wood. When he came to us, he could not walk.

Eric would only refind his desire to live when he could discover that he was loved by another person and that there were real and lasting bonds between them – not possessive bonds, but bonds which could liberate.

Because Eric was deaf and blind, this relationship could only be established through a touch filled with tenderness and respect, a touch which reassured him and showed him that he was supported and loved, that he was safe. It was important to spend a lot of time with Eric's body, bathing him, feeding him, walking and playing with him. Only through the constant fidelity of this touch could he gradually gain confidence and discover that he was lovable and able to grow, that he was valued. During the five years he was at l'Arche, Eric became more peaceful. No longer did he try, in a crazy way, to climb up every adult in his thirst to be touched. However, he still remained disturbed; there were still doors firmly locked within him, and his body remained rigid. We did not find the key which would allow him to open his heart and reveal his vulnerability and his capacity to respond with confidence to love. Perhaps that would have put him in too much danger. For to open his heart would have been to relive certain agonies and traumas of his early childhood, and particularly the experience of being abandoned; it would have meant accepting the risk of new failure in a relationship, a new abandonment. Would he ever have been able to take such a risk? We cannot know.

In another l'Arche community, Yvette was welcomed from a psychiatric centre. She was ten years old then and had suffered repeated rejection. She had always been called 'the mad child'. She hid the reality of her heart behind many aggressive and anti-social gestures. It took a long time for the leader of the community to meet her behind all those barriers. On arriving, Yvette was not ready to give her trust at the first overture. Those who have been terribly wounded, as she was, will not open up easily; they are suspicious of kind words, of kind people. Yvette did not want to live through another experience of desertion, so it was better not to create new relationships; she hid and closed herself up. Then, Yvette began to test the love shown her by making much mischief and by running away: 'Are you really concerned about me?' 'Do you really love me?' Then came the day when the innocent child within her dared to believe that she was loved. Yvette accepted the tenderness; she opened the door of her heart. However, very quickly she shut it again. But, for an instant, for the first time, she had tasted the joy of communion with another person. Some days later, she dared to turn again towards tenderness: she then began a game of hide and seek, a going and coming, until the day when she was able almost totally to open her heart. She had found peace. She had accepted dialogue. She had found trust in an adult. Today, she knows she is loved and appreciated; she is now 'at home'; she is learning to love and serve those weaker than herself. But it took much time and attention, much suffering and many battles before she was able to make the transition. During the dark days, the community leader, speaking of Yvette, said to me: 'In order for her to come out of herself and live, our hope in her must be deeper than the despair within her.'

Eric and Yvette needed a redemptive love. It was not simply a question of loving a child who has a handicap, but of loving a wounded child who had lost all confidence in self and in others, who was broken and entrenched behind barriers. Such children need a love which will put them together again and lead them to wholeness. Some children are so wounded that they are obliged to cut themselves off from their hearts and the pain of the past. They have built inner barriers in order to forget those agonizing times. However, in order to have a future, to have hope, all of us must come to terms with our past. The discovery of peace and liberation, and the possibility of growth, depend on the integration of one's being which includes the integration of the past. Some people are never able to do this; their wounds are too severe.

Redemptive love must permit children or adolescents to live through essential aspects of parental love which was denied to them. They must discover a deep and lasting bond with an adult. They must experience the joy that an adult has in being with them; they must discover that an adult has confidence in them, is proud of them and of their growth. This love must be very concrete and bring them back to a relationship with their own bodies.

Through this love these young people will discover the beauty and sacredness of their own bodies. They are able to discover this only through a touch of tenderness and forgiveness, a touch of immense respect and hope. Only when someone begins to be at ease with his or her own body, to consider it as their own, is it possible to approach a true relationship with the body of another person.

All of this will take a long time. Sometimes, despite every effort, it will never come about. The adolescent young man remains divided and disturbed and unable to find the right boundaries to relationships; or else he seeks too quickly a close physical relationship, which is always dangerous for him and the other person because sooner or later it leads to rejection; or else he hides behind walls which have been built over the years and flees from all relationships. In the face of this suffering, the most important thing we can do is to accept and continue living with the person, deeply respecting the wound that is being carried, but always keeping hope in our hearts.

THE ROLE OF THE INTERMEDIARY

In order to open oneself to others and to the world, a wounded person needs to find someone who agrees to act as an intermediary. When a true relationship is established, the barriers slowly begin to fall, the person is able to leave the prison of sorrow and fear in which he or she was enclosed. Discovering confidence in oneself, it is no longer necessary to fight others and one's surroundings. One can begin to have confidence in them too. Little by little, the capacity to listen, to welcome and to experience wonder grows, and one can open oneself to the universe in trust. The intermediary is like a rock upon which a person can lean, a source to which one can return to be sustained, confirmed and encouraged.

In the world of education, the intermediary plays a major role with the wounded person. They replace the parents when these have been lacking, those parents who should have been the first intermediaries; protecting, supporting, and awakening their child. To win the child over, the intermediary must approach gently, first creating a relationship of trust. The child must sense itself to be loved and respected by someone who wishes to live a covenant relationship, not wanting to manipulate, crush or impose, but wanting only the liberation and growth of the child. Before suggesting solutions, however good they may be, the intermediary must first discover the beauty of the wounded person, hidden under the ugliness and violence. In effect, love is not primarily to do something for someone, but it is to reveal to that person his or her value, not only through listening and tenderness, through love and kindness, but also through a certain competence and faithful commitment. Our challenge at l'Arche is to find and form those who will be such intermediaries.

THE EXPERIENCE OF GOD'S LOVE

A child who very early has an experience of God, will grow more peacefully and truthfully. This is even more true for the child or adult who has been rejected because of a mental handicap. Those who are able to discover themselves, either directly or through the love of intermediaries, as truly children of the Father, will be able more readily to drop those barriers which have been built around their vulnerable hearts, and they will experience a certain wholeness. To live an experience of being forgiven, washed in the living waters which spring forth from the heart of God, will, little by little, erase the feelings of guilt which are often so tenacious.

When a child has lived through unbearable suffering and has been obliged to close itself off behind thick walls, this meeting with God is less simple and clear. It may even seem that the walls around the heart prevent the meeting with Jesus. However, there are signs, tiny signs, which occasionally may be perceived, showing that Jesus is there, hidden behind the walls. He is the only hope in all these sufferings of the heart.

The religion of Jesus is truly good news. It is not, first of all, a series of laws which one must obey. It is an experience of the loving call of Jesus, a meeting with him in faith and tenderness. This encounter, which opens us to the universe and to the Father, reveals that we are precious in the eyes of God. The negative image we have of ourselves is gradually transformed. When we discover we are loved by the Father, we can begin to trust ourselves; our hearts are on the road to being healed. This experience gives hope. The call of God is within us like a seed; with other people we can grow in the Church, in the community of those who believe in Jesus and who wish to serve him in the way of the Beatitudes.

One of the great sufferings of all children, handicapped or not, is that the thirst to be loved is so exacting that parents are not able to respond adequately. All of us are wounded in our hearts; all of us have been wounded by our own parents and by life. We all have our difficulties with relationships, and barriers behind which we hide. Parents love their children, but they have their own fears. They, too, have been wounded by their own parents and by life. Sometimes they are not able to carry their child with tenderness. Their hidden aggressiveness manifests itself when the child passes their tolerance level. This is why it is indispensable that parents do not stand alone in front of their child. If they are alone the child identifies them as the source of everything, as God: he or she makes them idols that are worshipped rather than icons which signify the presence of God. The child is unable to accept that not everything in its parents is good. If, however, parents introduce their children to the mystery of God, the child will discover that parents are not alone and all powerful; they are not the prime source of life; they can have their faults. The parents are then able to ask forgiveness of their child when they make mistakes. The child and parents are together before God as brothers and sisters, praying and asking forgiveness together.

When a child discovers through a Christian community that it is possible to have a personal relationship with God, everything changes. It is no longer necessary to live the relationship with one's parents in ambivalence, expecting too much from them and blaming them when those expectations are disappointed.

Even if one is sometimes disappointed, it is still possible to love them. In discovering the fidelity and compassion of God, through Jesus who is the Good Shepherd who loves and forgives, who truly leads and supports each one, and who always remains faithful, it becomes easier to drop one's barriers. This love of God lived in the community of the Church is not a figment of the imagination, springing from a disillusioned and broken heart; it is truly an inner experience.

Not long ago, Donald, who has a mental handicap, said to me: 'During Father Gilbert's homily, my heart was burning.' Many people who have a handicap, and many children, have had this experience of a burning heart. Unfortunately many 'adults' don't believe in these inner experiences.

When the child discovers an absolute in relationship with God, it is possible to accept relativity in human relationships, especially with one's parents. The child discovers that interpersonal relations are neither ideal nor impossible. They are a reality which exists, but with difficulty, with many failures, reverses, hurts, but also a reality full of joy which is deepened through a thousand pardons and reconciliations. In this reality, the ambivalent and conditional relationship with its message, 'If you are good, I love you; if you are bad, I reject you', is transcended.

When a child experiences the absolute in relationship with God, then it discovers faithfulness, pardon, and the reality of a covenant relationship. Because of the covenant with God, covenant with parents and others becomes possible. Relationship is no longer based on compatibility, but on a covenant. Then the bonds between people are more profound than emotions, feelings and even capacities for love and hate. There, forgiveness is possible.

If God is not present, it is more difficult for the child to live the relationship with its parents as a covenant. Likewise, it is more difficult for a man to live a permanent and deep relationship with a woman, and for a woman with a man, if they have not discovered the relativity of their relationship. Neither will ever be able totally to fulfil the other; they are not God for one another. They both have their wounds, interior flaws, sins and infidelities. In order to live and deepen the covenant between them, to mutually accept the differences and limitations, they need to have confidence in the absolute of a relationship with Jesus.

LOSS, GRIEF AND THE LOVE OF GOD

Human life generally begins with a period of acquisition: in childhood and youth, one acquires knowledge, friendships, all sorts of goods. Then, at a certain moment as an adult, one begins to live a series of losses: diminished strength, health problems, loss of work, loss of friends, until there comes the final loss, of one's life. These losses mark sorrowful passages in a person's history which can sometimes be shattering. They are followed by a period of bereavement during which one enters, more or less, into the cycle of depression–aggression. But, after this time of grieving, positive strengths spring up again, allowing the person to accept the new situation and to move forward on the road of life in a new and creative way.

The particular drama of those who have a mental or physical handicap is that these losses come too early in life, before they have acquired the inner strength that would enable them to face loss. Sometimes loss comes at birth, or even during the pregnancy, when the baby is deprived of the love and esteem of its parents, affecting physical and psychic development. These losses and the grief which follows invade the life of the child prematurely, when it has neither the strength nor the human means to cope. Moreover, sometimes the child has to face a distress so profound that it can be overcome only if there is a deep inward experience of the love of God. In that love which burns, illuminates and enlivens the heart, one discovers that one is precious to God just as one is, in one's very being. That love gives meaning to life, it gives strength to continue living; it enables the person to break out of the cycle of sorrow and anger; it stops the flight into illusion.

I remember a mother who had lost her six-year-old son. She told me that when her son was three-and-a-half-years old, he had been struck down by a paralysis of his legs which, little by little, invaded his whole body, and he became blind. Some months before he died, his mother was weeping at his side. Her little one said to her: 'Don't cry, Mummy. I still have a heart to love my Mummy.' That small boy had attained a real

25

maturity; he knew how to give thanks for what he had, rather than weep for what he had not. Such maturity often comes from an inner experience of God which, I believe, is given to people who are particularly poor and who, because of their weaknesses, would not otherwise be able to continue living. But in order to receive this experience, the person in distress must be in supportive surroundings.

2

Education and Its Demands

THE NEED FOR A UNITED ENVIRONMENT

When an adult and a child find themselves alone together, the relationship can become dangerous for both. Healing the heart and moving toward personal unity is not possible through a relationship limited to two people. The adult risks becoming too attached to the child or not attached enough; and the child will become either too dependent or aggressive. If the attachment becomes, as it often does, too possessive, the adult, in satisfying his or her own emotional needs, is afraid of anything that could lead to separation. Through this, the freedom to educate, to be firm with the child, is lost.

The child is the fruit of a man and a woman, the fruit of an act of tenderness and of love. During the years of development, the child needs both man and woman, but it needs also that they be united to each other. If they are divided, the child will experience division within and will enter into a state of confusion. Just as the abandoned or inadequately loved child lives in a state of insecurity, so too does the child who senses conflict between its parents. In this insecurity, it is necessary to protect the heart by building barriers and creating an appearance of hardness and of autonomy and freedom. It is intolerable for a child who loves both parents to feel one parent rejecting the other, forcing the child in some way to choose between them. A natural consequence may be a vacillation between the two according to the situation, which can quickly become a game in which conflicts and the demands of education and growth are avoided.

When parents are in discord, the mother tends to depend too much on her son because she feels forsàken by her husband. Similarly the father tends to depend too much on his daughter

27

because he feels forsaken and judged by his wife. Only when the man finds a refuge and support in his wife, and the woman in her husband, are they freed not only to love their child, but to educate and help it to grow.

Certain deviations and sexual difficulties in a child arise from the lack of unity between its parents. The body of man is made to be united with the body of woman. The psychology of one is complementary to the psychology of the other. They are created to be companions and friends; they are made to have children and to educate them together. The gifts of one harmonize with the gifts of the other; their differences are enriching. If, at the dawn of life, the child senses discord, rivalry and even hatred between them, then the development of his or her own sexuality will suffer. There will probably be a deep fear of the opposite sex, and differences between the sexes will be seen as sources of conflict rather than as a potential for harmony.

The emotional life of the child whose father is totally absent cannot develop in a healthy way. The mother tends to seek in her son the fulfilment of her own emotional needs, because she feels abandoned by her husband and experiences an inner void; if she takes on the attitude of 'spouse' with her son instead of mother and educator, she risks warping the normal development of his sexuality and personality. The mother fears losing her son. She fears the eventual separation, in which, having already been abandoned by her husband, she will find herself utterly alone. Unconsciously, she wants to prevent her son from becoming attached to another woman. She creates in him a fear of separation from her, and a fear of other women, whose presence will engender anguish, obscurely reminding him of how his mother impeded his liberty and his desire to grow. He will be blocked in his relations with women, and probably never be able to live a unique relationship in marriage. Often there will be homosexual tendencies. A comparable situation in the case of a father with his daughter will similarly affect her ability to relate to another man.

Growth toward the healing of the heart and inner unity implies not only the attention of others, but the presence of a loving unified milieu. All that has been said in regard to the healthy development of children is even more vital for a child who has a mental handicap. When there is inner division, there is a tendency to project it on the outer situation. Thus the child exploits the flaws and weaknesses in order to manipulate others and to satisfy its own instincts, avoiding the efforts necessary for real growth. For the integration of its being a child must be surrounded by men and women who co-operate harmoniously. In order to find an inner harmony and to be at ease with his masculinity, the adolescent or the man with a handicap needs men who are at ease with their own masculinity. This means those who are able to have simple, open, true and unifying relationships with women without dominating them or being dominated by them, who are able to recognize in them gifts and qualities which are different from their own. The same, of course, holds true for women in order to be able to discover their femininity.

Without this unity in their environment the adolescent or adult with a mental handicap will be unable to assume the demands of growth and healing. A wound in the body heals naturally if the body is healthy. But the heart cannot heal itself, it must be surrounded by those who will call the person to go beyond him or herself.

THE 'YES' TO GROWTH

Gloria, of whom we spoke earlier, is now fourteen years old. Her mental handicap is slight. Before coming to us, she had been dragged into the world of prostitution. Emotionally she is terribly disturbed. Little by little, she became attached to the assistants of our community. Finding a certain stability, she began to be happy there. But, there was still a pull in her to her former life. The house leader said to me one day: 'Now, Gloria must choose. She must choose life or death, either to root herself here or to return to her former life; we are not able to make the choice for her.'

It is impossible to break down the inner barricade of another. Certainly, the love, goodness and firmness of adults who confirm and give security are indispensable, but the free compliance of the person, even if that person is severely handicapped, is also necessary. Here we touch the secret place of each one's personal freedom. Some people are attached to their blockages and their prisons; they prefer the familiar to the unknown. It seems easier to remain in the slavery of sadness, than dare to advance in insecurity along the road to liberation. Some pleasures, like drugs, briefly give a feeling of life, of well-being. Momentarily anguish is taken away. It is difficult to free oneself from these seductive pleasures which lead not to life, but to death.

To live with deeply wounded people solidly barricaded behind their iron bars is a battle! But we must not give up. We must fight on, with ever more patience and dialogue, ever more prayer. It also requires truthfulness, fidelity and the competence of professionals. It demands an ever deeper commitment. One cannot fight the battle alone. There must be a team, which is deeply united, to help the person say 'yes' to growth.

TENDERNESS IS NOT ENOUGH

The starting point of human growth is in welcome and love. The child's first home is in the womb of its mother, then it is in her arms. This is both a place of rest and a space where life is found. In the experience of love and protection, the child feels secure. All education is based on that welcome and the mutual confidence it engenders. Indeed, a child will make efforts only if it feels loved and respected, not treated as an object or as an inferior. If the child is a person with whom one speaks as an equal, he or she can be confident, knowing that someone has confidence in him or her.

Demands made on a child without appreciation and understanding of its inner being will provoke reaction. Feelings of anger and rebellion will rise up, even if they cannot be expressed openly. Adults will be seen as those who crush liberty and the fullness of one's desires. Law will appear dangerous. In fact, this happens when a father, instead of using his authority to free the gifts of his child, imposes his own will in order to use the child to fulfil his own needs or to satisfy his pride.

In the gospel of St John, Jesus speaks of the good shepherd who knows each of his sheep by name. This implies that he has listened to each one attentively. Jesus distinguishes between the good shepherd and the hired worker who runs away when he sees the wolf coming. The good shepherd gives his life for his sheep. The sheep have confidence in him because they sense that he truly loves them and really wants them to live fully, that he is even ready to sacrifice his own personal interests for them.

A child who has no confidence in authority cannot accept the demands it makes and the effort it requires. Confidence will be lost when there is ambiguity or a dichotomy between words and actions. A son is unable to accept the demands of a father who makes no demands on himself or who does not love and recognize the son as a person in his own right.

I remember a young man whom I interviewd for a television programme. He had lived in the world of drugs. I asked him to speak of his experiences. Then, I asked him what his parents thought of it all. 'They were furious,' he told me. 'And what was your reaction to that?' I asked. This young man, sixteen years old, looked me straight in the eyes and answered in anger: 'Sir, my father is an alcoholic.' This young man sensed a double message coming from his father which caused him to lose all trust in him. If his father had said to him: 'My son, don't be like me. I know what it is like to be a prisoner of dependence. Don't make yourself unhappy as I am,' the son would have understood and, perhaps, he could have accepted. That would not be a double message, but truth: truth demanded that the father be honest and humble.

For children to grow and acquire a true inner dignity, it is not sufficient to be loved with tenderness and accepted as they are. They equally have a need to be encouraged, strengthened and guided by a father or a substitute father, a true and good educator who believes in them and their capacity for growth. The father, or the substitute father, must prove to the child that it is truly loved and that he is interested in its well-being and development. Children who sense that their father is more interested in his own reputation, his work or leisure, or that their presence is a disturbance, will not heed their father's advice or guidance. Walls will be built between the child and authority.

THE CHALLENGE OF EDUCATION

In a sense, all education involves a struggle. The growth of a child or of an adolescent is exacting: it requires an effort. It is easier for a mother to wash her son if he has a disability than to teach him to wash himself. Education demands time and patience, especially when the child lacks self-confidence.

It is not easy constantly to call forth a person with a handicap.

It is not easy to find the right balance between listening and challenging to growth, or between letting the child be and constraint.

Liberation is the goal of all education. This implies both liberation from those instincts which enslave and impede living in truth and reality, and liberation to develop the gifts and the qualities of the person to the full.

However, these two forms of liberation can be realized only if the person has space to live and to grow. We are all like plants, requiring sufficient room to put down our roots. Plants need water, air and sun. Children need to be loved, to be supported and affirmed. They need environment which will encourage their growth and efforts, but they also need adults who will help them in the struggle against the powers of darkness and the refusal to live.

In 1981, I went to live at the 'Forestière', a home for ten people with very severe mental handicaps. I was astonished the first time I saw Evelyn throw herself out of her wheel chair. At that time, she was 19 years old. She is very handicapped mentally: she does not speak and has little control of her body. Only one of her arms works reasonably well. I stooped down to help her get back into her chair, but Marcelle, the assistant who was with her, stopped me. Marcelle then angrily told her not to act up like this and to get back into her chair. A struggle began between the two of them. Evelyn waited to see what was going to happen; but seeing that Marcelle was not going to give in, she began to crawl towards her chair and to try to get in it again. That took a great deal of effort on her part. It was only then that Marcelle began to help her get back into her chair. For many people with handicaps, it is so much easier to let others do everything for them than to try to do some things by themselves.

It is always up to the person in his or her liberty to say 'yes' to growth and to the efforts that this implies.

THE COURAGE TO FORBID

We live in a society where many are afraid of the demands of true education. There is a tendency to say that one must be tolerant and allow each person to fulfil their own needs, to follow their own ideas and instincts. At the same time, there is a rejection of oppressive authority, ignoring the fact that those who exert this form of authority have often themselves had an authoritarian upbringing. A person who, in childhood, was not helped to assume true responsibility, and was frequently crushed, will never be able to exercise authority well.

Education implies that one knows when and how to forbid. There will be a time to forbid alcohol to someone who is in danger of becoming an alcoholic. It may be necessary to forbid a man with a handicap to cycle in the village if there is a real danger he will hit someone or cause an accident. Similarly, it is right to discourage a woman from going out alone if there is danger that she may be molested or if she unconsciously seeks to be molested. One must prevent a man from striking or exploiting a weaker person. There are times when one must do everything possible to prevent someone from closing up in an inner world of depression or fantasy and to bring the person back to where the source of life and beauty can be discovered. All this takes time, love and great firmness.

If a relationship between a man with a mental handicap and a woman seems restricted to 'sex' without any real friendship, or if the relationship is not fostering the growth of either but, on the contrary, is leading them to new forms of despair, then one must have the courage to forbid it. To allow them to continue such a relationship would be to show a lack of respect towards each of them, and a lack of hope in their capacity to live in true freedom.

Sometimes, however, it is necessary to let a person 'burn their fingers', and even to touch the depths of their misery. For some, it is only through the experience of real failure that a dialogue can be initiated and growth can begin. It is not possible to grow to greater love if there is no space for error. The father of the prodigal son let his son go, knowing that he would probably do foolish things. All of us have so many illusions. Some believe they know everything; others that there is no danger, or that they will be able to extricate themselves from any danger on their own – they refuse to listen to someone more experienced. Sometimes it is necessary for such people to experience failure.

But, this way of learning is not always practical for those with a mental handicap, especially in the areas of alcohol, drugs, violence and the exercise of sexuality. We cannot allow them to destroy themselves or to destroy others. The risks must always be carefully weighed.

Freud talks a lot about taboos. It is true that in former times a religion of fear was preached. If one disobeyed the law, one was rejected by the community or one risked being condemned to hell. This can lead to neurosis. The religion of Jesus is a religion of mercy. Jesus came, not for the just but for sinners. He wants life, not death. Prohibition for a Christian is not the same as taboo. It is not final, and fear is not the prime motivation. Forgiveness and love transcend the fear. To prohibit is to help someone move towards true liberation. It is only one element of education. If we forbid something without a positive orientation toward some other alternative activity, we may crush the person, if they have neither the strength nor the motivation to conform to the prohibition; the attraction to the easy way out, to pleasure, to compensations, to the need to assert oneself is too strong.

EDUCATION OF THE HEART

What is true for a child is true for the young person or adult with a mental handicap whom we welcome at l'Arche. Many come to us without having received any real education. They have been trained at a psychiatric hospital or centre where they were obliged to conform to its laws through fear of punishment or the promise of privileges. But this is not true education; it is, rather, the way animals are trained.

Life in community requires the recognition of certain rules, the welcoming and respecting of others. If we want to be the centre of attention, to have always the biggest piece of cake, then we will live in a state of continual conflict. We will tend then to crush the weak, to search for companions who agree with us, to avoid all those who seem to oppose us. It is a struggle in which all seek their own interests and, in those interests, manipulate others. We cannot live harmoniously together if we are thinking only of ourselves.

This is what divides our society and our world, raising walls of fear between individuals and nations. The poor are crushed while more and more armaments pile up for defence or attack.

A human being who does not think of others and their needs, sows the seeds of division and war.

This individualistic attitude is the negation of love. It leads to sexual activity concerned only with selfish pleasure. It does not engage the heart in a true and harmonious relationship which expresses a real communion with and tenderness for the other, confirming and helping the other towards fulfilment.

The fundamental principle of all education is to open the heart and the mind to the needs of others. This implies a certain quality of observation and of listening. There is an education of the intelligence through concepts and knowledge. There is also an education of both the heart and the will in love and service to others.

The essence of education is to lead a person into relationships with others, in openness and sensitivity to their limitations and in response to their needs. Maturity is growth in responsibility for oneself and for others.

In the fourteenth and fifteenth centuries it was debated whether slaves had souls and whether they had a real inner life and were capable of making choices. Today, some people doubt whether a person with a mental handicap is capable of an inner life and of love. Some want to introduce a person with a mental handicap to sexual pleasure as a right, without helping him or her to discover the joy of loving and being in communion with another person.

The aim of education at l'Arche is to help each one to welcome people just as they are, to appreciate them, to see their beauty, and to respond to their needs for true growth and liberation.

Certainly it is important to learn to be autonomous. But, it is more important to develop one's capacities, not as an end in itself but in order better to enter into communication with others and to build with them – not against them – a world of justice where each one feels responsible for others. Those with handicaps are capable of such love. Maybe with the little they have, they are able to love more deeply than those who are rich in knowledge, power and possessions.

People with a mental handicap live closer to their hearts. Their perception and awareness are more emotional and affectionate than rational. On the other hand, people who have developed their reasoning capacities often have more difficulty meeting others freely. They live on the level of logic and competition, wanting to prove that they are the best. Intellectual faculties, powers of reason, and the capacity of action are often used to prove their superiority and to dominate others.

I do not believe that the capacity to give freely and lovingly comes only after a long development of the rational faculties. Certain theories of child development give the impression that the child is fundamentally selfish, only able to receive and consume. It is implied that until a more advanced stage of intellectual development has been reached, the child is unable to discover itself as a part of a greater whole. It is implied that gift of self is purely rational and willed. My experience with those whose reason and will are less developed gives no evidence they are unable to love freely and unselfishly, or that their hearts remain on the level of subjective feelings, incapable of union with another.

A newborn child lives in a profound communion with its mother. The baby receives and, in its own way, gives. The child loves and wants to express this love. It has need of its mother and the security she gives, but beyond this, there is an experience of a relationship with her. The child may not be rationally conscious of that love, but it senses the peace engendered by it. The child who is loved as a unique person, experiences a sense of well-being and the revelation of its own beauty, and is aware of receiving life and strength from its mother. The baby expresses its love through the gift of its joyful smile and confidence. The child, in communion with its mother, gives itself to her without reserve, without fear, confident of being loved. This in turn gives life to the mother, reveals to her her own beauty and the truth of her fruitfulness, her capacity to give life, not only biologically but spiritually, through love and communion.

As the child develops, its innocence, the joys of communion and wonder in the discovery of the world, are tarnished. In its vulnerability, its immense emotional need and almost infinite thirst to be loved, the child is wounded by the parents' lack of attention, whether deliberate or more often, unconscious. This opens the more profound wound in the heart of the child, that original flaw of which we spoke earlier. A series of barriers are then created because the feelings of inner emptiness, pain and anguish are unbearable. Yet, these barriers and even parental limitations can be positive, because they force the child to begin to separate itself from its parents and to work through frustrations. This becomes harmful only if there is a fragility too great to bear these frustrations or to overcome the anguish. Then, the child flounders in a sea of sadness. Alternatively, if the suffering is too great and too early, the response will be an attempt to cut off the pain and suffering and, in so doing, the deep feelings of the heart will be cut off. The defences thus built up become more or less impenetrable.

If the heart has been hurt, the child tends to turn toward knowledge, power and efficiency, toward personal success, indeed to all those areas which demand less relationship. No longer feeling unique in terms of love and communion, the child will seek to be unique in terms of action and production. Consequently, it will find it difficult to direct the gifts of intelligence and activity towards the service of others. The child will always tend to act in order to prove him or herself, to dominate, to feel superior, to compensate for the sense of inferiority.

When Jesus tells us that we must become like little children, he reveals what is most profound and divine in a human being. Behind all the barriers built up since childhood, there is the pure and innocent heart of a child where the gift of God resides. This heart is capable of receiving and giving love, of living in communion with another person and with God, capable of being a source of life for others. In the designs of God, it is the heart which is meant to inspire all human activities.

The great suffering and the great sin of human beings is no longer to believe in the innocence of communion and mutual trust which opens us up to others, to the whole world and to God. This sin is to let oneself be seduced by efficiency, power and material possessions rather than building one's life on love and welcome, with all the risks of suffering that entails. It is to close oneself up upon oneself.

Sartre, in his book *Being and Nothingness*, sees love only as a battle where one person wins and decides and the other loses and becomes dependent. He seems to ignore the reality of communion, which is different from 'fusion', which implies the disappearance of one or the other, or both. Communion is a union 'with' the other which respects, deepens and strengthens the identity of each one; but, this communion is only possible if we have had a true experience of freely offered love, where the other does not wish 'to eat us up' and make us dependent – a love which, on the contrary, helps us to grow and discover what is best in us.

So often people hide behind barriers of knowledge, power and wealth, fearful of relationships and dialogue. Love appears to them as no more than a manipulation or a desire to possess the other, preventing that person from being him or herself. Dependence seems to be a loss, a form of death. So, they harden themselves against this possibility and, in so doing, they hurt others.

LOVE AND THE PERSON WHO HAS A HANDICAP

In some ways, the masks adopted by someone with a mental handicap are often less marked, precisely because he or she is less rational and self-willed. Certainly, when a person feels alone and abandoned, he or she will react like everyone else. There will be a need to affirm oneself, to dominate and to win. Alternatively, the person will fall into a cycle of sadness, depression and anger, or want to prove that he or she exists through opposition and rebellion, crying out constantly: 'No, I won't!' But, if there is the discovery of being loved and believed in, that part of the heart which is most pure and innocent, and which searches for communion and celebration, will rise more quickly to the surface of consciousness. The person with a handicap is able to enter more quickly into communion with others, to love them in a spirit of self-giving.

Helping a person with a handicap to discover the source of life within needs someone who will call forth and awaken their innate power of love and communion. Often, someone with a handicap feels rejected; others see the limitations and the deficiency rather than the gifts he or she can bring to the human community. Who can believe that communion, compassion and welcome are human values when society constantly testifies to the contrary? In a world where one must be strong, must win and conform to the values portrayed in the mass media, the person with a handicap will always remain at the bottom of society's ladder, despite all the efforts of normalization. It is not surprising then that the person remains depressed and sad, struggling for a place and refusing to accept limits which society does not easily tolerate. Since his or her real gifts and abilities are often ignored by society, the struggle between the search for pleasure in a closed world and the desire to grow in love and service of others is all the more difficult.

In each human being there is, in an attempt to fill up one's inner void, this battle between egotistical tendencies, 'everything for self', and the opening up of oneself to others. This same battle exists in someone who has a mental handicap.

I believe deeply that the best way for those with a mental handicap to grow in their capacities for work and autonomy is precisely the acceptance of themselves, with their limits and capacities for growth, through the discovery of their capacities to love and live a real relationship and communion with others. It is sad when someone, refusing to face the reality of a handicap and afraid of the feelings of his or her own heart, closes up in isolation – for example, by living alone – in order to prove that he or she is 'like everyone else'.

At l'Arche – and at other centres too – a certain failure with this sort of autonomy has at times been experienced. John, for example, lacking other models, only looked for a well-paid job and a life where he could do what he wanted. Perhaps he had to acquire this kind of autonomy and the feeling of being useful, but the lack of authentic relationships and faithful friends soon reduced his world to work, beer and television. The isolation was perhaps a necessary stage in the discovery of a desire for communion and relationships, with all that implies. I am afraid that many who are mildly handicapped tend to close themselves in an autonomy which ends only in such isolation. On the other hand, we have also had some excellent experiences where handicapped people have found true autonomy and competitive work, but, pretty well always, they have also found peace of heart because they were in a network of good friends.

DEVELOPING CONFIDENCE

Education consists, therefore, in helping people to discover all that is positive and beautiful within themselves, and to realize that they can establish relationships with others, that they are lovable and able to love. They will discover then the joys of true friendship. They will also discover their human dignity, their capacity to work and to make beautiful things. Many of those we welcome have suicidal tendencies. They have an image of themselves which is so broken that they have no desire to live. We must offer them a milieu which will call forth what is best in them. Just as some environments call forth darkness and death, so others call forth life and the will to live.

One can deny something to another person only if, at the same time, one conveys an appreciation of and deep confidence in the other. It is the difference between a good shepherd and a hired worker.[1] Then, prohibition can be a sign of hope: 'I know that you can do better'. This presupposes dialogue in which the reason for the prohibition is understood by the one on whom it is imposed. Above all, it is of value when a person has a positive goal in life and can realize that this prohibition will help him or her to become more free and able to choose and find direction in life.

Education consists in supporting people as they begin to discover the purpose of their lives. There will be progress and failures and times of discouragement but, in falling, a person will get up again and thus there will be the discovery of forgiveness.

I remember a reflection by Dr Franko from whom I asked advice concerning Anthony, a very disturbed man who had committed a serious act with a child: 'You must go to see him and confront one another. He may be violent, for it is difficult to accept the darkness which he feels inside. But stay until you have both met and are reconciled. In the past, whenever Anthony did something bad, he was rejected and put in the hospital. It is crucial that he now has an experience of forgiveness.'

It is not easy to educate even a normal child, especially in a society where the values are seductive, materialistic and pleasure loving. Parents rarely have the time or the quality of listening necessary to understand their children fully. It is so much easier to put them in front of the television and give them playthings rather than to play with them and to do things together in joy and celebration. It is difficult for parents not to be possessive with their children and use them to satisfy their own emotional needs. Yet, it is even more difficult to be a good teacher and to

1. c.f. John, chapter 10, where Jesus distinguishes the good shepherd from the hireling, who is hired for the job and is only interested in the salary.

heal the wounded heart of a child who has a handicap, and to reawaken in it the desire for life.

TRUE AUTHORITY

It is not easy to be a good shepherd. I know the theory well and can talk about it. But I realize that often I am more like the 'hired worker' who needs to prove and protect his authority. So often I make quick judgements, forbidding or correcting without taking the time to understand what has really happened. When I correct at an inopportune moment and the correction rebukes rather than helps the other person, my action springs more from my own anguish than from a desire to help the person to grow. This happens most often when I have become overactive, when I have lost the source of light within me, when I am tired, or when I am far removed from the spirit of prayer, being too immersed in the daily concerns without sufficient recollection or inner resources.

It is not easy to exercise authority with love and in truth. One has to be firm and clear, and to respect the positive values of the person if one is to find the exact words and gestures which are going to help that person grow. I know my own weaknesses and fears in this respect. But, at the same time, I know the need of those suffering from a mental handicap to have someone who is deeply committed to them in love and respect, yet knowing how to be firm enough to ensure their development and the liberation of their gifts. The one who acts as a shepherd must be a rock of tenderness and truth upon which the other can rely.

I am especially concerned for those who in their early childhood had a bad experience with authority. When they have known only prohibitions without kindness or forgiveness, when they have had a rigid education without the stimulation or recognition of their gifts and capacity for growth, they have been deprived of life and development. Sometimes these serious blockages are apparent in their relations with authority, which they regard as a threat to their being. To regain their confidence requires much patience and goodness on the part of the one in authority.

The role of the educator, and especially of the educator of children and adolescents who have suffered traumas during childhood, requires a team where each member is mutually helped to be truthful, and to be true shepherds in their concern for the growth of each person. They become accountable to each other. It is very difficult to exercise authority alone; one so quickly becomes defensive or unconsciously oppressive. One tends to protect one's authority and the established order without permitting others to question it.

In order to be objective, a team needs an 'exterior eye', especially when dealing with someone who seems too difficult, disturbed or violent. It is hard to see one's own errors, especially when lack of attention and truthfulness are perhaps at the origins of violence or disruption. In l'Arche communities it might be the one responsible for the community, as distinct from the house leader, who plays this role. On the whole, we prefer it to be a person who has integrated the values of l'Arche within him or herself rather than a priest or psychiatrist – someone with experience of the suffering and needs of people, who has human wisdom and a knowledge of the Gospels. Priests and psychiatrists have a major role in the growth and the liberation of the individual and the community; but they must not seek to fulfil other roles.

In l'Arche, there is a danger that leaders do not have enough confidence in their own intuition, wisdom and educational abilities; they submit too passively to 'experts' and professionals. Of course they must seek advice from others who have greater knowledge and experience, but first of all they must assume their own role in truth and in trust.

EDUCATION FOR ADULTS

The education of a child is different from that of an adult, even if the latter has a severe mental deficiency. An adult with a mental handicap is, first of all, an adult, not a child. The body and spirit of a child are still developing, and so the child is naturally accepting and open. The adult already has a history, and the adult with a mental handicap often has a history of suffering and rejection. With a wounded image of self, there is too great a readiness to take the blame oneself. Such a person must be reassured, confirmed and supported. Perhaps there has already been some kind of training in the family or an institution in which different experiences, prohibitions or permissions have left their mark. Pain must be healed and bad habits overcome. At the same time, there must be dialogue, the acceptance of failure, and the experience of fragilities, mistakes and limits, in order to go beyond them.

Regarding the emotional and sexual life, the difference between the child and the adult is enormous. The sexuality of the adult is formed, often badly formed, perhaps even perverted by unhappy experiences in hospital, institution or family.

It is not easy to help an adult who has been wounded at the affective level to establish the right distance in a relationship with someone of the other sex. A man who has not been touched with love by his mother, or who has lived a long time in a hospital environment, is scarred in his affectivity. This makes him awkward in touching a woman, and this awkwardness leads to further rejection.

It is easy to touch a child with delicacy and tenderness. It is much more difficult with men and women who are disturbed. It is important to find ways of touching them in an acceptable manner, for example, when they are sick or complain of a particular pain. Or, it could be through friendly fights or in games and folk dances where there are precise rules about touch that must be respected.

When the values of l'Arche are opposed to those of the family of the adult with a handicap, the situation presents great difficulty. Paul's father, for example, spends much time in bars. Paul loves his father and imitates him. But there is real danger for him. He cannot hold his drink and his work suffers when he drinks. He senses the conflict between the values of his family and those of l'Arche. Similarly, some men and women go to their families and find their brothers and sisters, and sometimes their parents, having sexual relationships with different partners. We cannot let them follow the values of the family with all the likely consequences. At the same time, neither can we prohibit, as we would with children.

In this area there have been successes and failures. Robert, for example, comes from a family where there is much violence and alcoholism. He followed the same route even after he was placed with us. But after several years, he experienced a real healing. With the help of a group similar to Alcoholics Anony-

43

mous, he stopped drinking and now actively participates in the group. At some meetings, he testifies: 'I didn't know how I was going to get out of the hell I was in . . .' He is proud of his work and lives in a flat with three other men where he has found peace.

Alfred is a man who has certain capacities, but is emotionally disturbed. Refusing all help, he left l'Arche 'to live his own life' and ended up in prison. What will he do when he comes out? Hopefully having hit the bottom, he will be able to accept someone who will help him rise and give him confidence.

EDUCATION FOR EMOTIONAL AND SEXUAL LIFE

Education for emotional and sexual life means helping someone to have a sense of others, to be able to listen, to love and to have compassion and tenderness and, not least, to become responsible. True sexual education awakens the heart and helps someone move toward a mature affectivity.

This experience of awakening the heart needs a degree of identification with a parent-figure of the same sex.

The little boy imitates his father's relationship with his mother. The way the father acts towards women, especially his wife, will educate most powerfully the sexuality of his son. To some extent the same thing happens in a home for those with a mental handicap. They will act like the assistants or staff whom they love and admire.

It is through these relationships and the identification with adults that, little by little, people find their own identity. True sexual education takes place in an environment, a home, a network of relationships between men and women, where gestures and touch express joy and tenderness. Sexual education does not occur through anonymous pictures giving depersonalized information. Certainly, it is important to know the anatomy of the body, the times of fertility, the connection between the sexual act and procreation. But it is not good to show the sexual act through pictures or slides, which is done sometimes alas, because these images risk awakening a sexuality cut off from the life of relationship.

In reality, the role of an educator is to help adolescents understand and appreciate the functions of the body, and to answer their questions. It is serious when a person thinks his or her own body is bad. Counselling engaged couples will, of course, require more precise information as to how a man and woman live their sexuality together. But the emphasis should be on the importance of listening and respecting the differences of the other. Sexual education is not so much a practical manual of what one must do and how, as a basis for harmonious sexual relationship, but rather a matter of helping people to be at ease with their own sexuality. It implies a growth in the capacity to see the other as someone with needs. It also includes helping people to face the challenges and difficulties involved in relationships. This is, in fact, apprenticeship for true love.

At l'Arche I have noticed that often those who have the most need of sexual education are the assistants. They have been influenced by the mass media which trivializes sexuality and are unable to understand its true significance. They are afraid of the cry for affection from those with a mental handicap; they don't know how to respond to manifestations of tenderness or, still less, to manifestations of genital sexuality. Because they themselves are unclear, they are unsure whether to condemn or to ignore what they see.

In our times, we need more than healthy morals in this area of sexual relations. We also need a deep understanding of anthropology, which is the foundation of human and Christian ethics. It is necessary to help others to understand how sexual relations without true commitment are destructive of the human heart and that sexuality must be oriented, elevated and integrated by love, which alone makes it truly human. It is important to learn that this sexuality, prepared by biological and psychic growth, develops harmoniously and is realized in its fullness only by the attainment of emotional maturity, manifested in a selfless love and in the gift of self.

This form of sexual education is equally necessary for men and women with mild mental handicaps. For them, the influence of films and magazines can sometimes be shattering. The mass media stimulate their sexual instincts, arousing false dreams of 'love'. It is more difficult for them, because their hearts are more fragile than others and they are close to anguish and so easily influenced. They must be able to speak with someone about these questions and come to understand what is at stake in true love. Only then will they be able to make a real choice.

In this area of counselling and education it is imperative that the intermediary is a person with the great sensitivity and goodness needed to face so much suffering, confusion and hurt. Too rigid prohibitions, combined with punishment, can lead to greater guilt and fear. It may aggravate blockages or the search for secret sex and escape into erotic dreams. The intermediary must also recognize the boundaries of his or her role. It is not necessary to know everything. There must be respect for the private space and the inner secret of each person's being. It is right to interfere only when it is certain that the other is in danger. This rule is always the same: create a trusting relationship where dialogue is possible and where, little by little, fear disappears. It is true that sometimes it will be a long time before such a relationship is achieved. This requires people ready to commit themselves over a period of time and willing to accept the demands implied in such a commitment.

The exercise of authority and the use of prohibition in the sexual sphere is especially difficult. In fact, each educator or intermediary has his or her own wounds, difficulties, anguish and struggles. An intermediary who has to fight against his own homosexual tendencies will probably be more rigid and less sympathetic and understanding of the homosexual tendencies of others. It is so difficult to be objective in the area of sexuality where all one's needs and anguish are so easily projected. Those who desire 'free' sexuality for themselves may encourage others to the same 'freedom', not because it will help them to grow, but in order to justify and prove that their own attitude is right. Without clarity about one's own sexuality, it is impossible to be clear and true about the sexuality of someone else. Fear of one's own sexuality leads to fear of the sexuality of others and consequently to rigidity. Without the freedom to relate to one's own sexuality, there will almost certainly be misunderstanding of the sexuality of another. Those who do not believe in the possibility of their own growth in this area, will never have confidence in the growth of others but will fall into a legal and static vision. Those who do not acknowledge their own weakness, will not develop the patience needed to help others to progress and integrate their sexuality into their life of relationships.

MAKING THE NECESSARY TRANSITION TO GROWTH

As we have seen, a child sensing that he or she is not loved, experiences emptiness and anguish. Barriers are built around the heart to repress the pain. To cut oneself off from one's own heart is to cut oneself off also from all that is most profound and intimate within, from the very source of life and love.

Unable to live with others, there will be escape into cerebral activities, aesthetics, work, immediate pleasure and aggression, or even into the world of madness. Love is impossible. The intuition of the heart, which makes us sensitive to others and their needs, and which is the foundation of communion and mutual confidence, is lost.

How can we help people rediscover their source, their wholeness and centre of unity? They must be helped to descend through all the barriers to the most vulnerable region of the heart. In so doing, they will relive certain anguishes of the past, and certain experiences of hate and revolt born of all their inner suffering.

Contact with the deepest feelings of the heart is often an almost unbearable experience, unless there is a good and competent person who will listen to the cry and carry the suffering with compassion. This person must know how to accept the aggression which may erupt and is a necessary passage to a true relationship.

I am more and more convinced that each human being needs to be supported and accompanied in such a way, so as to grow and become more loving, transparent and responsible, and to break out of the prison of fear and anguish. It is not only the person with a handicap who needs to be accompanied through these interior transitions, but also the assistants. They, too, have their blockages and barriers and must learn to grow towards an ever more responsible love.

At certain times, someone who can no longer find a way to escape inner conflicts will enter into crisis. A crisis is the revelation of an interior void. This emptiness can be filled ultimately only by an authentic love, a love which comes from God, though it often passes through people. This true love alone reveals to the person that he or she is not alone but is precious, of value and capable of giving life and of loving. When the sources of life are awakened, there is an experience of wholeness which fills the void which the crisis uncovered.

In demolishing the barriers and refinding the sources of life, a measure of inner unity, of integration, is attained. Such transitions imply suffering. But often this suffering is accompanied by a new experience of God in the depths and vulnerability of the heart of the person.

The Relationship between Man and Woman

MAN AND WOMAN IN THE VISION OF GOD

The difference between man and woman is a radical and fundamental one which permeates the depths of their consciousness and affects all human behaviour. It is at the beginnings of life itself. In Genesis 1:27, it is said 'that God created man in his own image, in the image of God he created him; male and female he created them'. He wished that they be one, that they be 'one body'. (Genesis 2:24). Man and woman are complementary in their bodies and their psychology. They each discover their being in relation to God who created them; each in the image of God, they are called to become like God. Such is their fundamental, ultimate goal in the universe. However, they are also in the image of God in their union and their unity of love. Each one is with and for the other. Each one discovers his or her self in relationship to the other.

John Paul II speaks often of the 'sponsal'[1] or 'nuptial' body of man and woman, in order to emphasize that the body of one is made to be united to the other.

Man and woman, in the mystery of creation, are a mutual gift . . . they were united by awareness of the gift; they were mutually conscious of the nuptial meaning of their bodies, in which the freedom of the gift is expressed and all the interior riches of the person as subject are manifested.[2]

Genesis also shows that when man and woman turned away from God, when he was no longer present in their union, they

1. From the Latin 'sponsus', spouse.
2. Pope John Paul II, General Audience of Feb. 20, 1980, *L'Osservatore Romano* (English edition), N.8 (621), 25 Feb. 1980.

lost their primal innocence. They then experienced a terrible emptiness within themselves; they knew anguish; they became aware of their nakedness. It was then that the man blamed the woman and sought to dominate her. Their union was broken; they became rivals. They were no longer one body.

Thereafter, men and women turned in on themselves, locking themselves up in a closed world. Then they sought power and possessions to fill their inner emptiness. It is possible to open ourselves again to others, to create bonds with them, to enter the world of love, communion, and gift, of sharing and welcome, only if we are reconciled with God and discover his presence within us.

The attraction that man and woman have for each other calls them to go beyond another isolation, that of death. Above and beyond the attraction and the individual choice of one another, there is in the depths of man and woman a desire to give life to a new human being.

Sexuality is oriented to fecundity. Woman's body is made to be the first home for a child. Man's body is made to bring fecundity to the woman. Physiologically, the woman's sexuality is more interior, the man's more exterior.

Woman's body, because of its role in procreation, is less efficient for strenuous action than a man's. On the other hand, pregnancy and the care of children demand the greater part of woman's strength and energy on so many levels. Finally woman is different from man because she carries in her body a kind of bond with death: her ovaries, given to her since her beginnings, age with her. Her fecundity dies when she reaches her late forties or early fifties. Man, however, always produces new sperm. He does not experience this death of biological fecundity.

What exactly are the consequences of these biological differences in the cultural roles of man and woman? It is not easy to differentiate that which originates in the culture and that which orginates biologically, and what is the link between the two. At the beginning, taking into account the different functions of fecundity and material needs, it was obvious that man should give physical protection, going out to hunt, while woman was occupied with the home and the care of the children. This clear division of the roles carried a certain responsibility, peace and harmony. Each one knew what he or she must do; that facilitates unity! But, as we all know, it could also lead to division and to the oppression of women. This is what happened and what still happens in certain cultures, where men run the risk of being 'macho'. They have an image of themselves as the 'strong man', possessing several women without being responsible for them. The men don't work much; they drink a lot and often squander the family's money. These men are wounded and devalued by the scorn of the women. The women, on the other hand, are industrious and strong. Emotionally, they attach themselves to their sons, seeking support from them. The sons are used to being served and spoiled by their mothers and find it hard to leave them. Once they are married, it is always to their mothers they turn when in conflict with their wives. It is a vicious circle, resulting in a break between the man and the woman as friends and spouses.

Another difficulty, especially in the United States, but also in other industrial countries, comes from a certain ideal of social success to which the man is obliged to conform. All familial and scholastic education is geared toward this professional success, seen as a greater priority even than family life. In these societies a doubt hangs over the value of marriage as a permanent bond. This vision of man makes the woman insecure. She is obliged to harden herself in order to protect herself against the eventuality of being abandoned by her husband. She is not able to trust him, and feels the necessity of having skills which will allow her to manage should she be left alone. These attitudes inevitably sow seeds of division and mistrust between men and women. One can easily understand that the woman cannot bear this oppression and so takes any means to liberate herself from it. She rebels at the idea of being man's plaything or possession, and so refuses all dependence on him. It is understandable that some women go so far as to cut all men out of their lives: they strive to be appreciated not for their femininity, but for their intelligence and their professional and artistic abilities. They are obliged to accentuate their aggressiveness and their desire for success, and they tend to deny the sensitivity of their hearts which, like man's, are made for communion and mutual dependence. They seem to be driven, in an attempt to defend themselves, to adopt the same false model of masculinity, which is oriented towards individual success.

In Western countries, preoccupation with gain and success and conditions of work, together with other factors (such as the role of the mass media), have considerably weakened the family, and the idea of service has been partially destroyed. We have over-developed the assertiveness necessary for life and success. At the same time, the bonds which unite people in the family, the community, the parish and the village are disintegrating. People are more and more isolated from each other. And so a vicious circle is created: one must harden oneself in order to survive; but because 'the body' which is the family, the village, the community has been weakened, people who are non-productive and fragile (whether due to a handicap, age or ill-health) have difficulty in finding their place. They are quickly rejected. In a society where everything accentuates individualism, it is necessary to be first at something; if one is not first, then one is good for nothing. Thus life becomes a battle. It is necessary to be 'better' than one's neighbours, and this leads to a need to look down on others, scorning those who are not successful.

This obsession with being first encourages the strong to walk over the weaker ones. This has had repercussions on the family and on the relationship between men and women. Because he is exempt from the burden of maternity, man believes himself to be the stronger. He has a tendency to look down on the woman, who is taken up with material needs. He is able to work outside the home and to practise a profession. The woman stays at home 'producing children' and caring for her husband. Unfortunately, he then falls into the trap of these illusions. He believes himself to be superior, more intelligent. He no longer listens to the woman. She, like a slave or like a person with a handicap, is considered inferior. There was a time when it was even questioned whether a woman had a soul!

The consequence, or perhaps the origin, of these attitudes is the theory that the body is inferior to the soul, which is more divine, nearer to God or the gods. Man, more detached from bodily needs, not having to submit to the servitude of maternity, is therefore closer to God than woman. The works of the intellect and erudition are thought to be more 'divine' than mundane work; intellectual work and the liberal professions are 'nobler' than manual labour. White-collar workers tend to scorn blue-collar workers, to use them to enrich themselves at their expense and sometimes to crush them. The unskilled labourer has no voice.

Then comes the revenge: class war. The perspective is one of rivalry between the conqueror and the conquered, the first and the last. When 'the body', which is the community, is destroyed, it is exceedingly difficult to harmonize the different roles; people begin to take on the attitude of 'each one for oneself'! The Christian vision of man is very different from that of our industrial societies. The Word, becoming flesh, came to reveal the great dignity of *each person*, above all the poorest, and to call them to live in a community which is united like a body. The last are first. Its values are neither power, nor social influence, nor riches, nor human glory, nor even individual liberty as an end in itself. Its values are those of love exercised in the 'body'. Jesus was not an intellectual; he was a simple worker, son of a carpenter. His mother remained in hidden silence, serving the body of Jesus and the mystical body. In the Church, she is glorified and recognized above all the apostles and the priests.

In the perspective of Jesus, the weakest ones are the most important because they have the greatest need to be loved, protected and served. 'Blessed are the poor, for the kingdom of heaven is theirs.' The leaders, those responsible in the Church, are there to serve them, to wash their feet. God chose the weak to confound the strong, the foolish to confound the wise, the scorned to confound the proud. Jesus blessed his Father for having hidden these things from the wise and the prudent, from the intellectuals and the rich, and for having revealed them to the poor. Is not this the vision which the Second Vatican Council has, more forcefully than ever, proclaimed above everything else?

But whenever there is a perversion, when the body is broken, when man does not give woman her due, when the poor are not respected, it is difficult to retrieve the situation. I can understand the anger and suffering of so many women. What is to be done now? Is it really possible to continue living, as many do today, in this dynamic based on aggression and individualism? Or is it possible, through recognition of and respect for differences, to rediscover the deepest community values of trust and mutual support?

In the following chapter, I speak of the home. Today, when one speaks of the values of the home, men are bored and women get angry as if one wished to send them back to the kitchen and housework without any contact with the world outside. However, it is important to speak of the home, because in our times many families are broken, and so many children live with a sense of being abandoned and isolated. Consequently they are in anguish. They must harden themselves in order to survive, and their hearts, the most sensitive part of their being, are smothered, if not crushed. It seems to me that the most fundamental need of our society is not to have more teachers in the universities, but to have men and women who together will create communities of welcome for those who are rejected, alone and lost – and their number is legion. It is more than ever essential to rediscover the sense of home as a place of tenderness and welcome, where each one can find the deepest value of his or her being – the heart with its capacity to receive and to give. Today many people wish to become involved in society, but they live all alone and sometimes in conflict with others. They have neither community nor family as a source of personal nourishment, of tenderness and peace.

I am convinced that our society desperately needs the reconciliation of men and women in order to build community together. They have such need of each other, and it is painful and even dangerous when there is no mutual respect and appreciation of one another.

It is obvious that women and men are equally competent. Within l'Arche, women are responsible for some of our communities, men for others. Women, for the most part, exercise authority differently from men, neither better nor worse. At certain times in the history of a community, it might be better to have a man carrying the responsibility; at other times a woman. The essential is that neither exercises authority alone. Woman has need to lean on a man, and man on a woman. This complementarity is healthy and valuable.

In my experience, I have found that usually the man is more rational. He has a better sense of means, of organization, of structure. The woman is often more intuitive and her heart is frequently more sensitive; she has a better sense of ultimate objectives and of people. This is not to say that every community must comprise both men and women, or that a community of only men or only women will never be successful. If all the members of a community are of the same sex, then it is important that the leader of the community shares responsibility with others who in some way bring in this complementarity. There are some men who are more intuitive and some women who have a sense of organization.

Each of us, according to life, circumstances and inner disposition, may develop more of our feminine qualities (those which touch intuition, welcome, tenderness, caring) or more of our masculine qualities (those related to reason and organization). When necessary, men can be sensitive to the body and express great tenderness, just as women can do hard, manual labour. The important thing, in a family as in a larger community, is that each one is able to use his or her own gifts, knowing that the gifts of one are not better than the gifts of another, that each one at his own level participates in decisions, that each one listens to the others and cares for their well-being. That is the joy of community, which God wants for humanity.

Given the specific purpose of l'Arche, namely the welcome of people who have been wounded in their minds and in their hearts, we need both men and women assistants. They play complementary roles in the healing and growth of people who have a handicap, provided that they love one another and co-operate together.

ACCEPTING DIFFERENCES

The family is the primal community. It is founded on the difference between men and women and on the recognition of each by the other. Both are with and for their children. Children are also different but not inferior. Though they do not have the power of adults, they bring their own gifts to the family and to the community. They are more than just potential adults.

There is a tendency today to deny differences. This tendency is the basis of most sects, in contrast to the basis of community. A sect always wants uniformity, even a form of fusion, because this gives greater security. The leader has absolute power and is regarded as a unique and inspired prophet, even like a god. He or she is the sole reference, demanding unquestioning obedience. The goal of community, on the other hand, is the freedom and growth of each person. It implies the recognition of covenant relationships but in diversity. In community there is a mutual bond which still leaves each member free to grow in his or her differences.

To feel lonely and isolated because of being different is a terrible human suffering. Peace lies in the recognition of the value of differences. When someone feels alone, they barricade themselves behind walls to suppress the pain. However when a person feels accepted by others it is possible to drop defences and enter confidently into relationships with others. When bonds become firmly established community is born.

The Scandinavian countries introduced the notion of 'normalization' for people who have mental handicaps. This concept has value, if we understand it to mean that each person has rights and that no one must be excluded from the human community because of a handicap. But, if by 'normalization' we mean that everyone is 'normal', that everyone must be the same, then we deny differences, and this is wrong. People with a mental handicap are different in several ways. They have needs and gifts which are their own. What is important is that these gifts and these needs be truly acknowledged and that each person is able to find his place in the human community.

People having a severe handicap are unable to develop as human beings all by themselves. They need someone who can give them special support. They need to create bonds and to live with others in the spirit of a family. They do not want to live simply with professionals who, notwithstanding their goodness and competence, get paid for putting in their forty hours and then leave. They wish to live in true bonds of friendship with others.

When for ideological reasons we cannot accept people who are different, but scorn them or wish they were not present, this is intolerable, because we are forcing people to be other than they are. Only when differencees are accepted, not as a threat but as a treasure, is each one free to be him or herself.

But acceptance of differences demands a maturity of heart and spirit that human beings do not possess straight away. Instead of an authentic acceptance of the other, there is often the search for a symbiotic unity: 'We love each other', 'We are one'; but without truly respecting the other in his differences and his need to grow. Respect implies dialogue. It implies that we give another the space he or she needs to live and grow, that we do not invade his or her frontiers. Now the demands of recognizing another person in this way are onerous; they can be a terrible challenge and bring suffering.

In order to find one's space one often has to cry out or even fight for recognition. That can hurt those close by and arouse their anger. The search for symbiotic unity often comes from a fear of this anger. On the other hand, when differences are respected then the potential for aggression is acknowledged. If we want others to live, we must refuse to manipulate them or control their lives. We must, in fact, give them more space; and that involves suffering and loss for ourselves.

In order to accept this loss and all that resembles death, there must be, as I said in the first chapter, a new interior strength which comes from the experience of God's love. Without faith in a transcendent being, is it possible to welcome differences, and beyond that, to create real community, a 'body' as it should be, demonstrating a solidarity among its members which springs from their mutual recognition of the need each has of the special gifts of all the others?

The community needs those special gifts which are especially man's and those which are especially woman's; it needs the gifts of the child and those of the elderly; it also needs the gifts of those with a handicap. In the same way, the world community needs all men and all women, all races and all nations.

MIXED HOMES

A milieu with both men and women is the best and truest one for someone with a mental handicap. The woman calls forth in man that which is most profound: the heart, tenderness and sensitivity. The man thus becomes more gentle, more attentive, more discerning. He opens himself more to others. The woman awakens his goodness, just as the man awakens all that is most beautiful and feminine in the woman. Man and woman are as mirrors to each other; their differences reveal to each other who he is or she is. These permit each one to be himself or herself in his masculinity or her femininity. In a mixed milieu, work must be shared according to tastes and aptitudes; men and women more naturally find their own place and, through that, assume a clearer responsibility.

A man does not always call forth the best in a woman, nor a woman that which is best in a man. The presence of both sexes may awaken in a woman the desire to seduce, to play one man against another and so to create discord. She may awaken in a man real sexual obsessions. In one of our communities, a man was so disturbed by the presence of women that he became completely crazy and extremely violent. He found peace in an institution where there were only men.

For some men and women, mixed homes are dangerous. They reawaken such instincts of dependence, lust, hate and destruction that it becomes impossible for them to live close to the opposite sex. As we have said, there is in some people such a fear of love! I remember a prisoner saying to me, 'When someone is brutal with me, I know how to react; but, when someone is kind, when someone is tender toward me, I am lost.'

Some men and women have erected such enormous barriers around their vulnerable hearts, and have so learned to live with them, that attempts to remove these barriers can be dangerous. At l'Arche, we have met men and women suffering from 'hospitalisation', having lived so many years in institutions in a kind of anonymity with strict discipline. They are not able to live in a family setting where they are given freedom and are constantly faced with choices. They prefer a more structured life, less threatening to them. But, perhaps, more deeply they are afraid of the pain hidden behind the fortifications of their heart. They are afraid of awakening sexual compulsions which might be accompanied by obsessions and horrible jealousies, or by a desire to kill because the one whom they love is not exclusively theirs and theirs alone. If, in childhood, they have not had a special relationship with their parents, anything which awakens the desire to be unique could become a dangerous mixture of trust and fear, love and hate.

In most of the l'Arche communities throughout the world, men and women live together. I can say that on the whole, this seems to be very positive, bringing peace and harmony and helping most residents to integrate their sexual urges. In those homes where there are only men or only women, there appears to be more aggression. Mixed homes are more human, because people in them seem to be kinder and more sensitive towards one another. Nevertheless, it is still true that for some there must be homes only for men or only for women.

SOURCES OF RELATIONSHIP

If, out of fear, someone is not able to live a personal relationship of communion and gift, a friendship, with someone of the other sex, he or she will inevitably be disturbed at the level of genital sexuality. This is why, if we wish to understand the emotional and sexual life of someone with a mental handicap, we must go back to the origins of his or her relationship with the father and mother.

I was surprised one day when speaking with Pierrette, a young Canadian delinquent. She appeared to be very tough. She loved to wear leather belts and ride powerful motorcycles. But, behind this façade of toughness, was an extremely sensitive heart capable of true love. She confided to me that when she hated a man she went to bed with him. She delighted in having him at her mercy, weak, begging for her body. It was evident that unconsciously she was taking revenge on her father who was very weak, an alcoholic who never gave her the love and tenderness she needed when she was a child.

The relationship of the little boy with his mother, like that of the little girl with her father, conditions the relationships which, when the child becomes an adult, he or she will have with those of the other sex. Certainly, as we have said earlier, it is not a question of separating the relationship of the child with one parent from the relationship with both parents. He or she needs both. If these relationships have been positive, the adolescent will have fewer difficulties with whoever will be his or her spouse. A child who has lived with many foster mothers is likely to have difficulties in living in a permanent relationship. Sometimes, adults have a tendency to unconsciously re-enact the conflicts and sufferings they knew as children. In fact, the fears and traumas of childhood condition future relationships. They remain hidden in the unconscious, and certain events tend to reawaken them.

Karl Stern in his book *Flight from Woman*[3] shows that some disturbed men either put woman on a pedestal – idealizing her, seeing her as a model of purity – or they see her as the prostitute, the temptress. They are incapable of a simple relationship, one to one, with her. This inability to see her as a friend is not

3. Karl Stern. *Flight from Woman*, Allen & Unwin, 1966.

primarily a rejection of women, but a rejection of their own disturbed genital sexuality.

When a boy, abandoned by his mother, has not experienced the warmth and bodily affection he needs, all his body cries out for the touch of a woman-mother. This is the case of George who lives in one of our communities: he had an almost uncontrollable need to touch and caress women, to attract them to him. His need to touch and be touched was not primarily a genital sexual need. It was not in the literal sense a sexual urge; it was a cry of his deprived body longing to be loved and appreciated by a woman-mother. The body remembers the early deprivation of touch.

George greatly annoyed women, who did not like to be touched in this way, since his attraction towards them was inevitably mixed with certain sexual desires. Some psychologists get people with this kind of difficulty to regress to babyhood in the arms of a substitute mother. But this can be dangerous, for, while it is easy enough to lead some who have lacked love during childhood to this type of regression, it is much more difficult to bring them back from this situation. Such wounded people want to remain at this level, demanding more and more, an unfailing love without limits, and thus an impossible love.

It is important that the team around George should understand that he is seeking a mother and not a wife. It is dangerous when these two aspects become confused. In order for George to grow, he needs to live a harmonious and peaceful relationship with a woman who will not awaken his genital sexuality but who will pacify him and give him security and peace. He needs to find a woman who knows how to make maternal gestures, who knows how to take care of his body without putting him in danger, who knows how to care for him and his clothing, who knows how to spoil him sometimes. However, it is also necessary that this substitute mother is not the only one concerned with George and that she knows when to absent herself in order to avoid awakening in him a sexual desire which could be harmful. George also needs to relate to men, who will serve as models in their healthy relationship with women. If George is surrounded by such a team, perhaps his heart will begin to grow towards peace and maturity.

Many seem to ignore the fact that, underlying the sexual drive, there is, in the sexual attraction, the simple cry of a body longing to be loved and touched with tenderness by another. This cry comes from the depths of a human being and often, as we have seen, has its origins in childhood. The links which unite genital sexuality and this call to be loved, held and caressed are so profound that sometimes they lead a person to a state of confusion and fear. The cry for relationship gets mixed up with sexual desire. A person may then be very afraid of relationships, especially if his experiences of sexual urges have been disturbing. Such is the case of someone I know who had been put in a psychiatric hospital for many years because he had molested a girl. Thus can arise a fear of all relationship with the other sex; the person may then escape into other activities to shield the heart. This often creates attitudes of domination or aggression.

This escape can be positive in a way; the person deeply recognizes that his call to be loved is so intense as to be too dangerous and too confused. When one is a big strapping fellow, one can no longer play at being a little helpless baby. Those who have difficulties in relating must learn to accept them. They must try to distance themselves from their own cry to be loved. A community life where relationships are more structured is more appropriate to their needs. There they will be able to channel their energies into leisure activities, work and service to others.

In our times there is a danger of thinking that everyone may become perfectly healed and find perfect unity, in themselves and with others. This type of idealism is rampant everywhere. New therapies engender more and better illusions. And each new day, new techniques are born which will bring about this long-awaited healing.

Personally, I am more and more convinced that there is no perfect healing. Each human being carries his own wounds, his own difficulties of relationship and his own anguishes. It is a question of learning to live day after day with this reality and not in a state of illusion, and to accept the deep suffering involved in the attainment of emotional maturity. Admittedly, it is sometimes necessary to know how to find help from competent doctors and psychologists, but we must also learn to accept who we are and live with what we have, focusing our strength on those others who are in greater need and sometimes in deep distress.

EMOTIONAL MATURITY AND IMMATURITY

We often say that someone with a mental handicap has a normal sexuality. This is true if we look at genital sexuality as no more than a physical and biological reality, separated from the person in his or her totality. But is it possible to separate the genital sexuality of a person from the need for love? For surely it is in the emotional needs that the difference appears between someone with a mental handicap and someone who has a developed intelligence and capacity to reason.

In order to live a deep relationship, including sexuality in its more physical aspects, it is necessary for the person to have a certain degree of emotional maturity and to be capable of exercising responsibility and fidelity towards another. Personally, I believe that people who do not have a mental handicap as such, but who enter into sexual relations in their early adolescence, without having attained emotional maturity, can do themselves much harm. They carry in their bodies and in their psyches realities they are not able to hold on to and integrate into their affectivity. It is important to ask ourselves if precocious sexual experience doesn't hinder the necessary process of maturation of the personality. For me, this remains a serious question.

The person with a real mental handicap, has enormous emotional needs. It would be erroneous to believe that gestures of tenderness and affection spring solely from a need for genital sexuality. My twenty years of experience in l'Arche have shown me the contrary. Some people interpret these gestures, as though they are leading to an expression of genital sexuality, of which they are afraid. In the vast majority of these situations, these are natural and spontaneous gestures which simply express: 'I like you. I like being with you.' In some cases, it is true, these gestures may also be mimicry no longer spontaneous but an imitation of what has been seen in films.

Of course, there are those people who are more developed and who seek an expression of their genital sexuality. They need to be helped to grow towards an emotional maturity which will allow them eventually to form a deep relationship with a view to marriage.

Many people with a mental handicap have undoubtedly a great wealth of the heart. Their love, in its simplicity and tenderness, gives them an extraordinary liberty with regard to established conventions. How many times we have seen someone with a mental handicap greet visitors by saying: 'What's your name? What do you do? Will you give me your necktie?' A grown-up girl with Down's syndrome can look at a man with great tenderness and take his hand, or throw herself into his arms. If she did not have a handicap, such an overture and lack of reserve would probably be interpreted by the man as an invitation to more total physical union. But this is not the case. Her tenderness does not necessarily imply a search for a sexual relationship.

Her tenderness and her call for tenderness are terribly disarming; because she has the body and the beauty of a woman, she is able to arouse the sexuality of a man. Alas, it is not surprising that men and women with a handicap are so often abused. In a little pamphlet published in the State of Washington, USA (population about 4,000,000), it is estimated that in this state no less than 30,000 mentally or physically disabled people are sexually abused each year.[4] This is a startling revelation of the suffering, loneliness and anguish of those people who abuse them!

Some people with Down's syndrome express their desire to marry their nurse or teacher. We should not be surprised by this; many little boys want to marry their teachers. A four-year-old boy can also say he wants to marry his mother. This reflects a desire for total oneness with her, a fear of being separated from her – a fear of growing up. Such fears are linked to deep anguish. We find similar characteristics in those with a profound handicap and with an immaturity comparable to that of small children.

At l'Arche we see a young woman with a mental handicap in love with a male assistant and a young man in love with a woman assistant. But isn't this normal for their level of emotional development? However, this obviously does not imply that they should be encouraged to have a sexual relationship or to marry. On the contrary, when there is this immaturity any such relationship would be lived outside any real covenant with all the responsibilities it entails, and would simply encourage and aggravate their immaturity.

Over the years, at l'Arche, we have lived a variety of experi-

4. *Sexual Exploitation: What Parents of Handicapped People Should Know*, Seattle Rape Relief.

ences which reveal the different forms this emotional immaturity may take. Edith, a young woman of 22, is very seductive. She desperately seeks men and loves to see them fight over her. She provokes rivalry and jealousy. It is clear that she needs to grow and find greater maturity. She has not yet attained even the stage of a simple or healthy friendship.

In another l'Arche community, Micheline, a young psychotic woman, has totally captivated Bernard. He follows her around like a puppy. It is evident that the bond which unites them is unhealthy and not at all liberating for either of them. They are closed in on each other.

Francis seeks a liason with a girl because his mother is convinced he will be healed if he sleeps with a woman. So he seeks a woman, but it is in response to his parent's desire, not his own. He is still only a child in some ways.

When someone has a broken or negative self-image and does not love their own body, it is impossible to love the body of another. There are some women who find pleasure and excitement in attracting men. They are terribly lonely and sad women who crave to be loved, but are afraid of not being truly lovable. Through their bodies they seek to attract men and awaken their sexuality, but they are afraid of real relationship and commitment. It is important to prevent other people who are terribly immature from falling into the snare of seduction and relationships which may hurt and disappoint them.

Emotional immaturity is simply a yearning to be loved, to be touched, to be at the centre, to be seen as unique, but without making the effort to love, without a willingness to assume responsibility for the other. It is a desire for a totally consuming relationship, linked to a fear of separation and growing up.

This immaturity arises most often when there has been no true paternal presence. If the mother's role is to cultivate tenderness and a sense of being wanted and loved, the father's is to call the child to growth, to love and serve others in their turn.[5] This is why a real education implies the presence of both parents. The mother says: 'I love you. Stay with us.' The father says: 'I love you. I am proud of you. You are capable of doing beautiful things, of making others happy, Go . . .' Of course, we must not

5. c.f. chapter 2, p. 31.

be rigid in fixing roles. Each in some way assumes both roles, but generally speaking each accentuates one aspect.

What is important is that we do not confuse the immature call of someone who wants to be loved with the desire for a sexual relationship. We must distinguish the desire to find a mother who comforts from the desire to have a wife. A marriage in which the man is searching more for a mother than a wife often breaks apart when he discovers his responsibilities as a husband. To enter into sexual relationships when one is at this stage of immaturity can hinder growth to the ultimate stage where one becomes capable of loving, of serving, and of being responsible for the other. This is why it is dangerous to introduce people too early into a world where they experience sexual relations without responsibility.

HOMOSEXUALITY, MASTURBATION AND ANGUISH

Many of the men and women welcomed at l'Arche have lived through very painful human situations. The majority of them have experienced long periods in psychiatric hospitals or other institutions. Perhaps these times of institutionalization could not have been avoided. So many families are unable to respond to the needs of their children in times of great difficulty. During these periods these young people perhaps came to know a staff of educators and nurses who really cared for them with great competence and goodness. But they are often marked also by deep suffering at the level of their emotions and by the painful question as to why they were abandoned and removed from their family. It was during these times at the hospital that some men and women were perhaps initiated into homosexuality, sometimes in a brutal way.

Those who suffer certain inner brokenness and terrible crises of anguish become very fragile. The spirit and mind become confused and all sense of responsibility is lost. Such people are easily manipulated and are unable to take control of their own lives. They seek desperately to calm their inner agitation by every possible means. One of these means is the exercise of genital sexuality, whether alone or with others. If this happens, it is very difficult to free someone from sexual habits once they are established and impressed into the flesh, precisely because they are directly related to the anguish of an unfilled hunger to be loved and touched. These habits give a certain appeasement to that inner agitation for a short time. There is a feeling of calm relaxation and well-being.

This cry of those who have a terrible need to be touched, to be loved and to experience intimacy with someone, can become so intense that they are pulled irresistibly into sexual relations. But it is not so much the sexual relation and the pleasure attached to a sexual act as such which is important to them, but a feeling of togetherness, through the proximity of bodies, which appeases their anguish.

This leads me to speak of another form of homosexuality which is in a way embedded in the psyche and the physical make-up of a person. I cannot say that, at l'Arche, I have encountered homosexuality in its most absolute form, which is the attraction on the level of genital sexuality for someone of the same sex and a fear or frigidity in relation to all those of the other sex.

The causes of this extreme form seem to be very diverse (I have spoken of one of them in chapter 2[6]). I have had the opportunity on various occasions to speak with men and women who live in situations like this. I am always moved by the depth of their anguish, and I know that I cannot make any judgement with regard to them and their lifestyle. At the same time, as an educator and as a Christian, my heart and spirit refuse to say that nothing can be done, that there is no possibility for change, and that it is necessary to encourage these people to be who they are without guilt.

My fight for justice is a fight for the liberation of all human beings. I long for the rich to be liberated from the weight of their riches and their craving for more, in order to enter into the spirit of sharing. I long for alcoholic men and women to be liberated from their slavery; I long for men and women who thirst for power and domination without regard for the weak to discover true service. I also long for those who are imprisoned in homosexuality to find a free heart capable of loving someone of the other sex and becoming fruitful.

I too have my blockages, and each day I must work and struggle towards a greater liberation. I believe that Jesus has

6. See p. 28.

come to lead men and women to liberty. The only condition for moving toward that liberation is to open our hearts to God, to know and accept our own poverty and fragility and to seek help. Especially in these days, though perhaps it has always been so, it is very difficult to admit one's poverty, weakness and sin . . . We always want to justify and to prove ourselves. If we but knew the gift of God, that is to say, Jesus himself, and how much he loves us and wants to give us free hearts!

It is evident that liberation from homosexuality, like all liberation from the weight of egoism and self-centredness, can only come after much struggle and effort, undergone with the support of a community life and real friendship, and accompanied with sensitivity and dedication by professionals and priests. Perhaps liberation will come only after many failures, setbacks and sufferings, after many reconciliations and rebirths in hope.

Almost all the people I know in the communities of l'Arche who are attracted towards homosexual encounters have been initiated into them at a young age, in a psychiatric hospital or asylum. The 'older' played with them, used and exploited them. One person was even initiated into homosexuality by his grandfather. Such situations are particularly sad and are the most delicate to deal with. We must help these men and women to find freedom from these tendencies which close them in upon themselves. We must help them to transcend the terrible injustices of the past.

I would like to say something similar concerning masturbation. As with other kinds of genital sexuality, the modern tendency is to trivialize it: 'It is not important. It is normal, simply a question of adolescence. It will pass. Do not make a fuss about it.'

Adolescence is of crucial importance, because it is the time of growth to sexual maturity. That maturity is shown in a real commitment towards others, a commitment which is not just a running away from one's own suffering into the outside world, but one which springs from inner peace, harmony and the search for unity and truth within. Jesus said: 'Blessed are the pure of heart, they will see God.' That purity is a quality of love in the sense that one speaks of 'pure' gold. It is the fire and intensity of love, of service, of humility, of patience, and of goodness. Thus, to the extent that adolescents struggle for this purity of love, they will progress towards a true maturity and will be able to assume responsibility in the deepest struggles of our world.

The other day, I was told of a woman of thirty who had had great difficulties with masturbation since she was seven. She could not overcome these tendencies and lived with feelings of enormous guilt. It is probable that this young woman had lived, at the age of seven, through a traumatic experience, now hidden in the unconscious, that caused terrible anguish. It was this which made her take refuge in masturbation; it brought a certain calm to her inner agitation. Now, on the conscious level, there is a habitual link between the experience of anguish and masturbation.

Masturbation can be dangerous because it tends to close the person up inside a dream world. The maturity of a person is manifested by a capacity to face reality, to cope with it, and really to love and serve people just as they are (and not as we want or imagine them to be). When masturbation begins at an early age, there is a danger of the person being trapped in a genital sexuality directed not towards communion with another and the gift of oneself to another, but towards a subjective pleasure of self. Furthermore, masturbation being a solitary act, it can reinforce fear of relationship with others. It then becomes a vicious circle: masturbation aggravates isolation and loneliness and thus brings anguish, which the person then seeks to alleviate by masturbation. The aim of education is to liberate the person from such an impasse.

I spoke of Gloria. Her parents considered her mad, but men in the area desired her. She left prostitution but there remained within her terrible struggles and compulsions. The assistants in her community have been able to stop her from masturbating in public. But at night, she manipulates her body in masturbation. For the moment, the assistants say nothing about this because she cannot handle too many prohibitions at a time. She is beginning to trust the assistants and to feel at home. This is an enormous step. With time, it is probable that the anguish will diminish. The assistants have also decided to give her something to help her sleep because the anguish at night is sometimes too awful. If she is able to sleep better over a length of time, this will help her to break the habit, because there will be less experience of anguish. What is important is for the assistants to accentuate all that is positive in her, all that gives her life and joy, all that awakens new and constructive energies in her, all that will bring her security and the feeling of being loved.

In our communities, there are also men who have been attracted by children, either to touch them sexually or to show their genital organs to them. These situations are rare, but they do exist and call for enormous vigilance. We must protect children from such traumatic experiences and we must help the person with a handicap to find real healing. We must also protect the community, for these situations could create a scandal with the neighbours and a court action against the community. In prisons, I have met men, maybe slightly deficient intellectually, who have been sentenced for sexual crimes and are often persecuted by other prisoners because of them. I am very moved by the suffering of these young men who are unable to control their sexual impulses and who must spend long years of their lives in prison. At the root of their wounded sexuality there is often a broken family and very often a break with the father. Alas, it is always the same story . . .

THE SUFFERING OF PROSTITUTION

Some time ago, I had occasion to speak with Father André Marie Talvas, who founded, in France, a movement for the reintegration of men and women who have been involved in prostitution. His movement, called 'le Nid' (the Nest) began when Father Talvas met a woman in distress in 1937. She lived alone, was sick, alcoholic and rejected by others. He did not want to leave her in her loneliness. Gradually she found life through him. Now, throughout all the big cities of France, 'le Nid' comes to the aid of those living in prostitution and other marginal people. Father Talvas knows a lot about prostitution and the suffering and needs of these men and women. He confirmed deeply my own understanding of the emotional and the sexual life. 'The plan of God for man', he told me, 'is to participate in the life of God – Father, Son and Holy Spirit. It is to communicate with another; it is to love. The greatest tragedy for a human being is to be locked up in oneself and unable to communicate. So many of the women I know did not receive their share of love when they were little. A person who has not received her share of love, will never be able to have her share of life.'

This is the suffering of men and women reduced to slavery and considered as objects. Yet there is also the suffering of their clients. 'Most of them', Father Talvas said, 'are searching not so much for sexual pleasure as for tenderness and communication. Often it is the poorly loved who seek for someone who will listen to them and welcome them. We cannot separate genital sexuality from the heart and the emotions. Beneath the search for genital sexuality is a longing to be loved. One seeks it where one can. We must help these clients – as well as the pimps and go-betweens – to find the true life of a couple which is at the heart of the true life of a family.'

In order to be liberated from prostitution a man or woman needs to find someone who will really respect and care for him or her, and will recognize what is truly precious and beautiful in them. Andrée, a victim of prostitution herself, said she was liberated when she experienced for the first time in her life that someone cared for her.[7]

After twenty years of life in l'Arche, living with people who are often very disturbed, I know how important it is to be aware of all the nuances and complexities in this area of healing and education. We have certainly experienced failures, yet each one has taught us something; the suffering, the anguish, of each person in distress is so different. It is true that there are basic patterns which are constant, but at the same time we must recognize that there are no fixed or precise laws. This is the reality of each human person and of his or her growth.

In order to grow, each person needs to be surrounded by friends and to be regarded as full of potential for growth. Deficiencies of love in early childhood play an enormous role in asocial and maladjusted behaviour. But sometimes chemical deficiencies accompany affective deficiencies. It is evident that there is an intimate link between the physical and the psychological.

Inner liberty and the attitude of those around us, the

7. She describes this in 'D'une réalité écrasante à une vraie vie: réflexions sur la prostitution', in the review, *Femme et Monde*, published by Le Mouvement du Nid, National Secretariat, 7 rue de Landy, 92110 Clichy, France.

individual's psychology and experience of faith, are all inter-related. We cannot say that the disturbance in a person comes solely from a lack of spirituality or fidelity, from a deprivation of love, or a chemical deficiency requiring medication. Anguish is a complex reality which has a physical basis and psychological and spiritual elements. For the heart and the person to be on the road to healing there must be a gentle and subtle harmonization of these different aspects.

4

A Place for the Heart

ACTIVITIES OF THE HEART AND ACTIVITIES OF WORK

There is a duality which exists between man and woman as they are called to form, from their two distinct bodies, one flesh. This is similar, in a way, to a duality which exists in each of us between the activities of the heart and the activities of work, which must be united in one person.

We have seen that passion for work may come from a fear of relationship or a fear of genital sexuality. It can be an escape, a compensation for anguish. It springs from isolation and leads to isolation. When individuals have no confidence in being unique in love, they seek to be unique in power and domination, or they fall into sadness and depression. When the heart is denied, there is a risk of giving primacy to struggle and competition in which it is necessary to win at all costs. But in order to be first, one has to step on and trample down others. It is hard then to be in a relationship of equality. One has to be superior, otherwise one is automatically inferior.

The role of ethics is to orient human activities to the service and the well-being of others, activities which otherwise would be inspired by egoism and a growing preoccupation with self, one's own power and pleasure.

There is certainly a danger at this time, and perhaps at all times, of separating the sphere of the heart and the sphere of work. In the family we live relationships of love and we even accept that morality and religion have a place there. But we do not easily accept the intervention of religion and morality in the areas of work and of the sciences. Here there is only the brutal logic of facts without regard to whether they crush or oppress. As we separate these two spheres, we reinforce a breakdown

72

in the human being and do not move towards the restoration of a lost unity.

At l'Arche, some men and women with a mental handicap grow towards a human equilibrium through work and professional activity which gives them a sense of their responsibility and dignity as workers. It is only in discovering this dignity of their being that they are able to advance towards a healing of their hearts. There are others, however, who must move to a healing of their hearts before being able to discover their ability to assume responsibility at work.

AT HOME

In order to attain a certain fullness and maturity, the human person has need of both work and a family. Work is the place where one's intellectual and manual abilities are exercised for some useful and beautiful purpose. The family, or community, is the place where the heart flourishes. It is home, with all the nuances which that word carries, that is so much more than walls of a house. It is 'my place', which implies security and privacy and, above all, relaxation and friendship. In work, there are inevitably tensions, for there is a finished product to be made, and perhaps a programme and discipline to be respected. At home, one relaxes and rests and finds nourishment. One is at ease with others, who do not judge or demand too much. They communicate tenderness and friendship and allow one to be oneself. Home is the place of the family, where people love each other, pray and celebrate together. It is a place to welcome friends.

Human beings come from the earth and return to the earth. They follow the rhythm of nature, in which there is day and night, work and rest, a time to be nourished and a time to exert energy. There is daily routine and times of celebration. There is winter, spring, summer and autumn. Each time, like each season, is important. Human beings are not disembodied spirits, but have bodies subject to the laws of nature.

I must admit that in living with people who have a mental handicap, I have been led to discover my own humanity. As a naval officer, I had to be quick and efficient. In war you have only seconds to sink the enemy ship before being sunk yourself.

Later I obtained a doctorate in philosophy which formed my intellect. But it was through living in a community and deepening my Christian faith that I discovered all the dimensions of my heart. In this area, those with a mental handicap were truly my masters. They led me to discover the beauty, joys and suffering of community life, with the daily routine and celebrations. They helped me to discover the value of the home.

The home is an extension of the body, a place where one is revitalized and where one communicates with others. If it is a place of conflict, where no one shares or communicates with others, it is intolerable. One has to run away to a bar or to another's home or into conjugal infidelity.

My experience has shown me how important the woman is in the creation of home. Woman has a profound sense of the nest – she carries her child within her for nine months. For example, she may have an intuitive sense of the right décor and furniture for the house that a man does not always have. Often she has the special gift of giving the house a soul.

Unfortunately, in our era and in Western civilization, we attach great importance to having a beautiful house – beautiful at least to the outward eye – a house where one's possessions are safe, but which often lacks a certain quality of family life. Then the house is no longer a place of celebration and tenderness where one loves to welcome others and make them feel at home. It is like a boarding house which we long to leave to go on vacation or to outside entertainment. And, because we are too tired to share with each other and have lost the taste for celebration, we passively watch television.

At l'Arche most of the men and women we welcome have never had a home. They had been placed in hospitals or other institutions. They have never experienced the joys and warmth of a family. Even if they lived in a family, they have been hurt by rejection and misunderstandings. This inner pain or trauma breaks down something inside them and often prevents normal psychological development. A few, however, find it normal to leave their parents, like their brothers and sisters, to work and live at l'Arche. All of them have a need for 'family life', for a comfortable bedroom where they can hang their pictures and posters on the walls. They need their own bed, their own wardrobe and a place for the things that are precious to them.

At the beginning of l'Arche, the local authorities wanted to force us to have a communal kitchen for all our homes. The state would finance the construction of small homes if we would have a communal kitchen because, they said, meals would be less expensive. We had to fight for each of our houses to have its own kitchen despite all the inconveniences and the costs. Twenty years at l'Arche have confirmed the importance of the family kitchens, and personalized meal-times in each home, for the healing and the growth of people with wounded emotions. This is true for the assistants also. The kitchen and the dining room table are privileged places for friendship, celebration and relaxation (and, contrary to state expectations, meals are less expensive).

If one does not have a home, one feels the pangs of loneliness, and runs the risk of becoming aggressive or depressed. The heart is not at rest. One becomes hyperactive, running around all over the place, seeking distractions, unable to listen, without inner peace. One runs the risk of destroying oneself and others.

Those who put most of their energies into work, overdevelop their aggressive qualities and do not give enough time to family, community, and the spirit of welcome. Their hearts are in danger of atrophy. This lack of balance in their lives will affect their sexuality.

Home, however, is not always a particular place. I know a woman who lives alone and whose work demands much travel. One day she said to me: 'I am like a snail. I carry my home on my back.' Some people are comfortable with themselves. They have found a meaning to their lives, and a certain wholeness or inner unity. They have their friends and people they can turn to. They don't need another 'house'. I believe that this woman had also found that God is her home and that she herself is the home of God.

Family or community life is the special place in which we come to know ourselves in truth. In political and social struggles, the enemy is always outside ourselves. We can identify who and where the enemy is. We want to be victorious and believe we are right, the elite. In family and community life, however, we quickly discover that the enemy is within us, preventing us from being open and able to share. It is the enemy within who incites us to jealousy, infidelity, egotistical attitudes and blockages. To live in a family or in community is always humiliating for our

ego which wants to excel. We quickly discover our darkness and
faults and how much we need to grow and to be forgiven.

Thus, the home complements the world of work and social
activity. It is the place where one can live covenant relationships.
It is essential for growth towards wholeness

THE CHALLENGE OF L'ARCHE

But for a l'Arche house to become truly home, it is necessary that
not only those with a mental handicap, but also the assistants put
down roots there. If the assistants are always changing, they will
never really develop bonds with those who have a handicap,
without which they in turn will not be able to put down roots.
There will not be 'a family'.

At l'Arche, it is not only a question of living with people
having a handicap, but of living with them *as a family*. This
includes giving them the chance to voice their opinions and to
participate in decisions. It is a question of living with them, not
according to a hierarchy of power, but in a community, a 'body'
where each one really has a place.

This is the challenge of l'Arche. There will always be those
with a handicap who are in need. But will there be those who
are ready to live with them as in a family? To live with an
anguished man or woman whose emotional life is shattered can
cause a lot of anguish in the assistants as they come to discover
their own limits and wounds. Many residences and centres have
begun by welcoming people in deep distress and without family.
They started with the hope of living a full community life
together, but little by little they have become institutionalized.
The assistants, who at first lived as a family with those they
had welcomed, have reduced the time which they spend in the
residence considerably. 'It is just not possible to live together,'
they say. They have been 'burnt-out' by the tensions, the lack
of support and of spiritual and intellectual nourishment. Will
l'Arche succumb to the same fate? Will we be able to find the
resources and life-style which will allow assistants to put down
their roots in the community and to live together with men and
women who have been rejected?

People with a mental handicap who are at l'Arche gradually
do become rooted. If they come from a family where they were

well accepted, they will, perhaps, have difficulty in putting down their roots with us, as they may still long to be with their parents. Sometimes, too, their parents, even though they are happy to have found a solution for their child, have difficulty in accepting that he or she has found a real home in l'Arche. One cannot have two homes. I know a young woman with a mental handicap who lived from Monday to Friday in a Canadian residence (not a l'Arche house); she also had her own flat, and went quite frequently to live with her father. Such lack of unity cannot be good. In order to grow humanly, there must be one special place for the heart and the emotional life. If there are several places, there will be a dispersal and lack of unity which is not conducive to growth towards wholeness.

Home implies a personal choice. Many who come to l'Arche do not have this choice. They are placed with us by their parents or a social worker. It takes time for them to find a certain peace and unity in their being and to discover who they are and what they want to do with their lives. After a few years, it is important for them to be able to choose to stay in the original home or to go on to another. This implies the need for a number of homes or apartments in a community so that each person can, if possible, choose his own home. I began the first l'Arche home in 1964. By 1966 we had welcomed, into the home eight men. Eleven years later six of the eight men had chosen other l'Arche homes and the seventh was living independently.

SEXUAL DIFFICULTIES WHEN ONE HAS NO 'HOME'

Children who are born into a loving family have an 'earth' into which they can put down roots. They know their origins and they know they are loved. Family is the place where they can grow and their hearts can flourish. However, slowly they discover that this home is too small for them. They need to leave in order to grow and to discover the world. They leave to find work, and to partake in social and religious activities which open them to broader horizons. They leave to find companionship, and perhaps to find a spouse.

Thus a new family is founded, a place of rest for the heart, a place of tenderness, of celebration and of forgiveness. It is a place which can become the springboard for other activities elsewhere. The love and peace of the heart which is experienced at home must be spread further. One works not only to earn money but to help other men and women to live in dignity and peace, to have their own 'home' which will be a source of life and a place of renewal for them.

I have noticed that those who do not have a home often develop sexual disorders which are almost impossible to overcome. I remember a single man who told me about his terrible need to masturbate. He often decided to stop, but the more he struggled, the more disturbed and tense he became. Finally it was impossible for him to keep his resolution. Masturbation became a means by which he relieved tension. It was a vicious circle. In speaking with him, I discovered he led a hyperactive life without any leisure or time for real relaxation. He was on the go from morning to night. He had friends at work, but he did not have a home in the real sense of the word. Nor did he have friends with whom he could relax. I suggested that he try to find a more harmonious and human life-style, one with less stress and with times where he could invite friends to his home, eat with them, waste time with them. This would perhaps ease some of his anguish. When we ignore our heart, sexual drives tend to mount to the surface to remind us that we are not disembodied spirits. This is not to deny that the fundamental problem is the anguish and guilt which were at the root of his hyperactivity.

I am uneasy when I see how some priests live. Their house is like a hotel, a place where they sleep and where they work. It is not a home, a place of relaxation, of welcome, of rest and prayer. They are hyperactive men who run about doing all sorts of things, but they don't seem to have any anchor. Their whole being constantly cries out their need for a place of repose and celebration. Of course, for consecrated men and women their place of repose ought to be prayer – long moments spent with Jesus, in communion with him. But in order to live this life of prayer, we have need of fellowship full of warmth and tenderness. If we have neither fellowship nor communion with God, the heart runs the risk of hardening itself or exploding in anguish. Both the human body and the human heart have exacting laws which must be respected. Human beings have need of a family, of a home, where life is good.

If so many people with a mental handicap have emotional

and sexual troubles, it is often because they feel ill at ease in their homes and, even more so, in institutions. In order to integrate our sexual instincts, we need the tenderness of a family or the warmth of a community.

In 1981 I attended a congress in Lyon, concerned with 'Handicap and Sexuality'. I was horrified when a member of the staff of a large Canadian hospital with 600 beds for people with severe mental handicaps, explained how he sought to initiate his adolescents and his young adults into an active sexual life. He taught them to touch one another. To me, it was so evident that this was not what the young people needed. Their need was not for a hospital – where they were necessarily anonymous and felt abandoned – but for their family or a new family, for a welcoming and compassionate home. These young people obviously experience feelings of rejection and live in anguish. They need a substitute father or mother, who will touch their bodies with tenderness, who will welcome them, confirm them, and who will recognize their value. They need brothers and sisters, friends and companions. Because they are deprived of a warm milieu and of loving and permanent relationships with their parents or with another adult, their bodies cry out to be touched. It is necessary for the staff of that hospital to respond to their cries and to give them friendship and tenderness. Their need is for people who are commited to them. In a hospital it is rarely that another handicapped person can give the secure friendship which they need.

Alas, often the family is not adequate for those with a mental handicap, who often receive the impression that they are a disturbance. They cannot find their place. They know that their brothers and sisters are admired for their progress in school or at work; they see them leaving home and getting married. They get the impression that they are superfluous. Despite all the efforts of the parents, it is difficult for those with a handicap to integrate themselves into the normal family rhythm. There are so many things that they cannot share. Conversations are quick and often too intellectual, and no one has time to explain. Visitors may not adjust to the slower rhythm they need.

When people are not part of a family and, above all, when they live isolated lives because of a broken self-image, they are forced to live in anguish. This is, as we have said, the most terrible of human sufferings. It becomes imperative to find

79

compensations which will calm this interior turmoil and bring a feeling of well-being, if only for a few minutes.

Escape from this anguish is often sought through the use of alcohol, or drugs, or in hyperactivity. The most frequent escape is in various kinds of sexual relations. But all these compensations are never able to fill the heart. Each time they deceive and, finally, they increase the sense of isolation and, therefore, the anguish.

As long as one is not sure of living in a loving environment, one harbours a doubt in oneself and there is anguish. There is a fear of being oneself, or showing one's true self for fear of a new rejection. There is the constantly nagging question: 'Is it possible that someone can love me for myself, or must I always appear interesting, seductive, capable and rich. At first, I seduce you and you come near to me. But is it not true that in living with me you will discover who I am and then leave me, because you cannot bear the reality of my being?

This is the terrible cycle which ends in despair. Is it possible that the day will come when we will discover faithful friends who accept us just as we are, with our fragilities and our gifts? It is then that we will come to accept ourselves as we are, we will let fall the barriers which we have built around our fears and vulnerabilities. Then we can live a covenant, a commitment with others.

A SENSE OF BELONGING

The first thing that someone with a handicap, and indeed everyone, needs is to feel at home. It is the sense of belonging to a group and of finding one's place there. Someone who feels a burden on others, or feels welcomed only out of pity, cannot feel at home. This is often why those with a handicap need to leave their family and to live in a community better organized and structured to meet their needs, and with a rhythm of life adapted to them. Those who find a community where they feel truly at home, where they are loved and respected and where they have a special role and responsibility, will progress in the integration of their beings and the pacification of disordered sexual urges.

I often hear of centres where men and women with mental

handicaps are encouraged to have sexual relations with others and exert 'the right' to sexual pleasure. I am convinced that, in most cases, this encouragement is an escape on the part of the staff from the demands of presence to people who are mentally handicapped. Those with a mental handicap need, above all, to have their own home, integrated in a small town or neighbourhood, where they live with those who will create community with them.

Community life, with its celebrations, its sharings and its love, gives a sense of belonging and security. I remember one day in 1968 when l'Arche bought a new home in the village of Trosly. I met Simon on the street. He is a man with a profound handicap. He said to me, 'I hear we bought the house on the Square.' He did not say, 'L'Arche bought . . .' or 'You bought . . .' but '*We* bought . . .' That 'We' is significant. Simon has the sense of belonging to l'Arche; he has found a new family.

When one feels a sense of belonging to a group, it is easier to espouse its values. Community life is not a hotel where temporary sexual encounters may occur. It implies common values, including those values related to the expressions of love. Community life implies clear options: one is either married or single. If one is single, one does not live as a couple; one lives only as brother and sister. So, in a community, the period of engagement or courtship, whether it be between assistants or between those with a handicap, is not easy, because they are between two situations; they are not yet married but they are moving toward marriage.

Community relationships resemble the relationship which exists between brothers and sisters in a family. This is a simple, deep relationship, full of affection, where each complements the other. But, obviously, it excludes a sexual relationship.

This matter becomes delicate when there are people in a community who refuse to adhere to the values of the community. They reject this aspect of belonging and want to form a couple outside the bonds of marriage, implying impermanence and instability. In such cases, there will be a threat to the foundations of the whole community life, destroying the dynamics of a group based on fraternity.

THE REFUSAL TO BELONG

At l'Arche, experience has shown us that community life responds to the needs of the vast majority of people having a mental handicap. However, there are some who cannot accept this sense of belonging and the values of community.

There are those who come from hospitals, or even from their families, for whom this community life with its slower rhythm, the place it gives to each one, and its celebrations, seems too wonderful. It cannot be for them. They are too broken. They feel too guilty, too angry and are convinced that no one is able to love them because they are too 'bad and ugly'. They need time to test love, to discover that it is possible to be loved, that the community is truly theirs.

There are those who are too greatly shattered and whose defences are too strong. Community life with its tenderness, its celebrations, and its call to relationship with those of the other sex, puts them in danger. It touches too much within them. It becomes a place of anguish and suffering, and they are obliged to convey this in gestures or actions that indicate they are unable to belong to the group. It is necessary for them to leave, but they do not know how to say this or to show it. Often they are violent or they are anti-social in order to be sent away. Some refuse to be in l'Arche, because they cannot stand being separated from their parents. They refuse to have confidence in others because this would imply an acceptance of their situation away from Mum and Dad.

Finally, there are those who, strictly speaking, do not have a serious deficiency on the intellectual level. They are at l'Arche because there is no appropriate institution to welcome them. They suffer most of all from a lack of education, of personal nourishment and support, and therefore lack confidence in themselves. They have been classified as deficient by mistake, and excluded from other avenues of welcome and education.

Some of these people are able to accept the community in the hope that it will be a springboard to help them go further. Others refuse it because they cannot accept being identified with those having more serious handicaps. In various ways they show their disagreement and desire to leave.

The community, with the help of professionals from outside, must try to decode these different refusals to belong. The 'no' may be a sign of a deeper 'yes'. It may also say: 'If you truly want to love me, come and look for me.' The 'no' may say, 'I cannot bear this life; it is too dangerous for me', or: 'This life is good, but I am not deficient. I am capable of living my life on my own and founding my own community or family. You must recognize this and help me to go further.'

I remember Germain. From the moment of his arrival at l'Arche, and for many years after, he refused all community services. He hid in his room or went outdoors alone. Fortunately, the person responsible for the home did not force him to do the dishes or participate in community events. Actually, Germain was not really deficient on the intellectual level, but he is epileptic, and his divorced parents could no longer keep him. They placed him in an institution which sent him to the psychiatric hospital because of his crises of violence. These were messages which the institution did not know how to decode. Germain had a very negative image of himself. He wondered whether he was sick, violent or crazy. In fact, none of these images corresponded to the reality. Germain was a victim of injustice and incompetence in the educational sphere. His refusal to belong to the group was a healthy sign. He was indicating his desire and capacity to be independent. Today, Germain works as a plumber. He is still a little unsociable. He lives in a small house with another man who has been along a similar road, and they are entirely responsible for themselves.

Jean-Paul had had a similar background. But his refusal to belong was less clear. He would say, 'Yes, I will come', from fear of causing pain, but he would not come; he had 'forgotten'. Jean-Paul is gentle and the image he has of himself is certainly less negative. Later, he too left l'Arche to live in an apartment. Several years ago he found competitive employment. Last year he married.

THE GREAT NEED OF THE HUMAN HEART

The great question in each of us is: 'Am I of value? Is there someone who believes enough in me to be concerned about me and to live a covenant relationship with me?' This is a cry for bonds of friendship and recognition which are lived in different ways.

There is the cry to be loved by a father and mother who know how to hold one in one's weakness. It is a cry which springs from the fragility of the infant or the insecurity of the adolescent. It is the cry of the adult with a mental handicap who needs tenderness, welcome, kindness, compassion, personal nourishment, support and encouragement. It is a cry which says: 'I need you. Your love gives me life and roots.' It is also the cry of every human person, because each of us carries our fragilities and our difficulties. Each of us cries out to be loved by someone who will support us. It is also the cry which turns us to God.

Secondly, there is the cry for a friend, an equal, a brother or a sister. One is no longer a little one who is loved but a person able to love and make another happy in community life. This desire for friendship may become a search for the unique friend in love and marriage.

Finally, there is the call to be a friend to the weakest and to serve. This call is answered in paternity and maternity: parents give life to the child and the child gives life and joy to the parents.

In fact, these three cries of the human heart are at the origins of the different covenant relationships between people, and are deeply linked together. They are always present, but in different proportions. One is not able to be a father, if one does not know how to be a son. A break in one of these covenants affects the others. These relationships constitute the network of affections in which each of us must live and grow. They are the milieu of life which keeps each of us from falling into isolation.

In order for a home to be truly a home, these three kinds of relationships must be found there. In our community on the Ivory Coast, Seydou was the first person to be welcomed. He was 50 years old, a Muslim from Niger. This man of great sensitivity and kindness had been placed in a psychiatric centre because of depression caused by several misfortunes which had occurred in his life. He died several years later, killed by a truck as he walked home one night. At the time the community welcomed Seydou, some children were also welcomed. The different ages brought something deeply human into the community. A community often needs grandparents and grandchildren. The mixture of different ages, strengths and weaknesses, gifts and individual qualities gives harmony to a family. There is a special peace and a balance to the emotional life of each one. These differences help each person to find their role and all help one another to live more fully.

The house and the family living there are the soil in which children find life and security. It is there that they are formed. Their lives are centred around their parents, who protect and educate them. Little by little, as they grow and develop, they find their centre in themselves and are able to leave their parents, to join with another and to give new life, founding another family, another home.

Between the moment when one lives with one's parents and the time when one creates a new family with another, there is a very rich period of adolescence. Young people search and become conscious of their bodies, their strengths and abilities.

During adolescence one lives at home, but it seems too confining. There is the risk of being smothered there. So, the individual puts one foot (and sometimes two) outside the home. It can be rather agonizing, like being between two chairs.

What does this mean for people who have a mental handicap? Of course, it is good that they have a place for the heart and where they can put down roots. But they too must not be smothered there. It is not easy to find a balance between roots and fruits, between security and insecurity, between comfort of home and the fear of growing.

They may live in a residence, which is not a community but resembles a boarding house or a hotel. The rules are too rigid, so they seek refuge elsewhere, perhaps in the home of a companion or in sexual encounters. If the community is too warm and affectionate and does not leave enough space for personal growth, then the person runs the risk of being stifled and of losing some of their vitality. A community is able to give life, but it is also able to hinder it. This is why a home welcoming people with a mental handicap must be very open to neighbours, friends, new assistants and visitors. There is a great danger if it closes in on itself. It is necessary that those who live there have more and more friends from outside who come to visit them. The community must be a home, a place of tenderness and security. But it must also be a place which is a springboard or an oasis of nourishment enabling those who can, to go on to a new stage in life.

5

The Community: Place of Sexual Integration

Many of those who come to l'Arche from institutions have suffered in their bodies and their hearts. They have been neither accepted nor loved; in their fragility and anguish they can neither accept nor love themselves. Hidden within is a profound, and sometimes violent, anger which is terrifying because they are not always able to control it. The first stage at l'Arche is generally a time of putting down roots, a time of finding peace and a sense of sharing. This time of healing is often long. It requires authentic relationships in a warm familial community and also work, which gives the person a sense of his or her dignity and reveals those capabilities which have been latent or ignored. In this way a person can break out of the vicious circle of being closed in upon oneself. In discovering the need for others, who also have their joys, pains, needs, the person is able to live and share with them a covenant relationship.

An ability to join the 'body', which is community, implies that the person is willing to make the transition from 'the others for me' to 'me for the others'. The decision to love and to take on responsibility is a fundamental choice to which all human beings are called. This choice must be accompanied by continuing efforts to grow beyond selfishness and the world of darkness and fear, which is in each one of us. Certain seductions, certain events in life can reveal the powers of fear. Every day, we need to make these little efforts to remain centred on growth in love and service, on the community, and on the source of the community, God himself.

Many in l'Arche have made this transition from being closed in on themselves, and the resulting death of the heart, to welcome openness, life. When she came to one of our communities, Vivian was wild. She was ten years old, blind and autistic, and had spent nearly all her life in an asylum. She had never experienced a permanent relationship, a covenant. In the asylum, which was a difficult place, she had been able to survive certainly, with a lot of pain. Coming to us she experienced more pain to begin with: she was with strangers and was even more insecure; anguish surfaced into her consciousness. She screamed continously. She ate her clothes and smeared the walls with her excrement. She severely tested the team of assistants who, by their love, their unity, and by the grace of God, were able to respond to her insecurity. Gradually, over many months, she discovered she was loved and she began to feel secure. She remains fragile, still having trouble with relationships, but there is a peace in her face and body, a sign of the resurrection of her heart.

But, many people do not make such a spectacular transition. They continue to carry their disappointments, their anger and their frustrations, which have their origins in childhood and which they are often not able to express. Such people have not really changed, though perhaps they have begun to move toward a sense of sharing or have found a certain dignity in work. In some sense, the community has become their home. However, their wounds are deep, and they continue to live in suffering and instability.

DREAMS OF MARRIAGE

It is not surprising that many of these people seek a refuge in dreams. The greater the wounds, the more they need their dreams, especially when the community is not able to respond to all their needs. A community is never perfect, but is a human reality: this naturally implies weakness and fragility. Some of those with a mental handicap will be dissatisfied, even angry, with the community, which, because of its own inadequacies and because of the depths of some peoples's wounds, is unable to respond to their cries. Thus, they dream of an ideal place, a place of rest where they will be totally loved and where they will be the centre of attention. They dream of perfect happiness.

Pierre had encephalitis when he was a child; it left him with one good leg and one good arm; he has a real mental handicap

as well. He compensates for his physical disabilities by a flood
of words. He dreams of being a radio commentator. When
someone feels impoverished, diminished, they tend to flee into
the imagination. How do we make a link between an intolerable
reality and an inaccessible dream? Between the loneliness in
reality and the loneliness in the dream?

Claude is very much at home in l'Arche and appreciates its
values, but he is still sensitive to the desires of his mother.
Sometimes his mother and l'Arche are in conflict over decisions
as to where he will spend his holiday, or questions related to his
health or his diet. It is not easy for Claude; he is caught between
two stools. How can he escape? He is forced sometimes to escape
into dreams. There, in some way, he can be himself, away from
the conflicts.

It is very important to see the different roles dreams can play.
The dream may, in some cases, open someone to reality and
love; in others, it may cut someone off from reality.

A dream is a sign of health; it shows that life is stronger than
death. To have no dream can be hell, a sign of utter despair.
The dream, like psychosis, is a refusal of death; it is a way of
reacting to inner pain. It is important therefore not to shatter
the dream too quickly on the grounds of putting people in touch
with reality, a reality which may be unbearable for them. When a
physical handicap constantly reminds one of one's powerlessness,
reality can be unbearable. At the same time, to allow a person
to be buried in the world of dreams is in some way to confirm
them in isolation. This is the tragedy of those who take drugs:
even when they are together, each one is terribly alone,
imprisoned in a dream.

The dream does not bring happiness, but sometimes it allows
someone to live and to survive. We should not disturb someone's
dream unless we love him with such tenderness that he discovers
that reality is not hell and that he has a place there.

One of the difficulties which confronts a handicapped person is
the image and the myth of marriage in our society and culture.
So much publicity is based on the image of the happy couple;
the films and magazines so often present that marvellous
love which brings happiness. These are the images which a
person retains rather than those of the pain of separation and
infidelity.

It is not surprising that so many handicapped people dream of marriage. For most of them, the couple is the only model they have. To become an adult, to be free and 'normal', is to marry, like one's brothers and sisters. Their own celibacy seems to them a sign of their handicap and inferiority. If they refuse this inferiority and wish to be a whole man or woman, they have no choice; it is marriage or, at least, the formation of a couple.

I remember Frances. She was twenty-three years old when she came to us. She was intelligent but walled up behind psychological barriers. It was a tremendous suffering for her to be separated from her family. Shortly after a weekend visit to them, she refused to eat and became almost immobile. She became bedridden and when the situation worsened she had to go to hospital. Several weeks later, she died. I discovered that during that last weekend with her family, in a crisis of violence, she had thrown out of the window the picture frame in which there was a photo of her younger sister on her wedding day. I think Frances died of grief, despair, and jealousy over her younger sister's happiness, a happiness which seemed denied to her.

Many men and women with a mental handicap dream of marriage because they dream of being 'unique' to someone, and of living in intimacy with that person. Their bodies remember the lack of tenderness in their childhood.

To dream of marriage is to dream of being queen or king of the feast, to have one's own home and space in which to live; it is the dream of being in paradise. Is not the wedding feast the great dream of humanity, the sign of the kingdom of Heaven?

It is important to interpret what someone who speaks of wanting to marry is actually saying, especially a person who has no friends. I asked Pierre, for example, what marriage meant to him. He answered: 'Oh, it is to have a wife to help me.' It might mean: 'I want to be like everyone else. I want to be like my big brother so that my parents no longer scorn me.' It could also mean: 'I no longer want to live in a community. I want my own home.' Or again it might mean: 'I want to be loved and seen as someone special.'

We must not underestimate the sufferings of those with a mental handicap when an assistant marries. I was painfully aware of this when Bernadette married James. Several men in the home were upset, not only because of the marriage, which was a state inaccessible to them, but, above all, because Bernadette whom they loved was leaving them. They were jealous of James; Bernadette preferred to live with James than with them. I understood how they suffered from this. Yet, obviously Bernadette had a right to live her own life, and to follow her own calling.

COMMUNITY AND CULTURE

People with a mental handicap are inevitably influenced by the values and ideas in their immediate surroundings with regard to relationships between men and women, and sexuality. Similarly they are influenced by the mass media with its concept of marriage as the source of perfect happiness, and by the often contradictory values of their families. These have formed their imagination and it is not surprising therefore that they live in a certain amount of confusion.

In fact, the surrounding culture is itself ambivalent. Through it comes the dream of humanity – to be happy, to live with ties of love; but it also shows the isolation and anguish of those who live for themselves, seeking to fill up the void in their heart by material possessions which lead them to struggle, to compete and, often, to be violent. This culture is very seductive. It captures the deepest energies of a human being. At l'Arche, we find people with a compulsive desire to possess things. Community life, on the other hand, based on listening and sharing, is a school for growth in love and communion. This new culture, founded on the Gospel and the Beatitudes, is directly opposed to the surrounding culture and commercial propaganda.

However, despite the powerful seductions of images and publicity, I am amazed by the qualities of goodness which one finds not only in those with a mental handicap, but in each human being. The human heart is fragile, falling easily into the snares of seduction: but it also desperately yearns for authentic love, lived in a bond of tenderness and peace with others. The human heart always recognizes the authenticity of true love even if it is sometimes afraid of its demands.

The illusions projected by the mass media and publicity leave an emptiness in the heart. They do not ease anguish and the fear of isolation, but rather augment them. They arouse, but are not able to satisfy, the heart thirsting for presence, communion, and infinity.

L'Arche, like other communities and so many families, wishes to respond to this most fundamental need of human beings. It wants to be a place of authentic 'rooting' where each one can find the deepest meaning of life and the flowering of his or her personality. It wishes to help each one to live the bonds of unity in a depth of love where all, especially the weakest ones, may find their place and carry a certain responsibility for themselves and others.

But, l'Arche is not a ghetto. The surrounding culture has formed the conscious, and often the unconscious, world of each one of us. This culture has pervaded each one of us, and through us, the community. This forces us to clarify the direction in which we orient our lives. At the same time, it may increase certain sufferings, keeping certain wounds open. Those who are frail and anguished have need of structures and solid references which our modern world rarely provides. On the contrary, it often augments anguish, isolation, fear and lack of trust in one another.

The challenge of community life is precisely to offer an alternative which responds to the deepest human aspirations; such an alternative, however, is not possible without an interior struggle. 'The truth shall make you free,' Jesus said. Yet, we are afraid of the truth and the responsibilities which liberty brings. This is the challenge of all education. Nevertheless, our experience of community has shown that the values by which we try to live have truly helped men and women to grow in their inner selves, to find meaning, direction and hope in their lives.

INTERPRETING BEHAVIOUR

L'Ange et la Bête[1] is a recent booklet on the findings of parents and educators on the sexuality of people with a mental handicap.

1. By Alain Giami, Chantal Humbert-Viveret, Dominique Laval. Publications of CTNERHI; Distributor PUF, Paris, 1983.

It is the result of a study of sheltered workshops and group homes in Paris and its suburbs. The first part shows the naivety of parents who are not able, or who refuse, to look at the sexual needs of their children. The second part of the book shows how educators focus on the genital sexuality of men and women with a mental handicap. The title of the book, *The Angel and The Beast*, is revealing. It is so easy to deny genital sexuality or, on the other hand, to separate it from the totality of a person's being and their most fundamental needs.

Educators must learn to look at this totality in each person. They must also listen to the cry of the person and be able to decode different kinds of language. When someone is violent, that violence is a cry, an expression, a form of communication. We must try not only to stop the violence and pacify the person, but also to understand what the violence is saying and decipher the message it contains.

At l'Arche we have discovered, in interpreting acts of violence, that they can be a cry for attention, or a cry of revolt against an injustice or frustration. This cry is more frequent in homes where there is little celebration and animation and where personal contacts are missing. This violence is in fact provoked by assistants when they are not really present or creative. Perhaps they are tired, or tied up in their own problems or tensions. In such cases, it is not so much the person with a handicap who must change, but the assistants. This is difficult to say and to accept. They, too, have the right to be themselves with their wounds and their sufferings. Of course, the person with a mental handicap must change too. Violence is not an appropriate response to a lack of attention, and all of us must learn to live with a certain level of frustration.

Not long ago, Richard had been reprimanded unjustly. He was furious. He went to his room and tore up three one-hundred franc notes. Talking with me later, he said: 'Three years ago, I would have been violent, now I just tear up money.' I believe this is progress, especially because he was able to verbalize it afterwards. But the assistant who reprimanded him unjustly must change too.

When Simon becomes violent, it is often because he has received a message from his father: 'Do not come home this weekend.' Simon suffers from this, all the more so because his father now lives with a new wife, and this has thrown Simon into confusion. It is more difficult for him to contain his emotions and to channel his anguish. He is more fragile than Richard and needs more attention from the assistants.

It is equally important to decipher the gestures of genital sexuality. The booklet, *L'Ange et la Bête*,[2] shows how the subject of genital sexuality is an area of conflict within institutions and between institutions and parents. This is inevitable, because of different values and because of the personal sufferings and sense of guilt within both parties. Genital sexuality becomes the focus of the conflict. The authors show how attitudes towards genital sexuality are ambivalent and often carry a double message.

> Permissiveness is held up as the ideal by many educators, but such advocates of permissiveness always speak in general terms which are rarely practised in specific and complex situations. To exercise restraint on those with handicaps is seen as repressive, yet these same educators argue the need for restraint in response to social convention and the compulsive sexuality of some mentally handicapped people.

In their article, 'Les besoins non couverts du jeune handicap adulte,'[3] Dr Stanislas Tomkiewicz and Dr Elizabeth Zucman speak of the opposing views of some specialists and parents. The former place less emphasis on the emotional needs of the handicapped and more on the genital sexual needs which are seen by them to be stronger than those of non-handicapped persons. They even describe their sexual urges as being rather bestial. For the authors, there seems to be a contradiction between the permissive ideology of the specialists and their rather deprecating attitude to the sexuality of handicapped people. The authors then go on to point out the confusion this attitude causes in those who have a handicap, especially if the handicap is slight. One the one hand, they are told to practise moderation, to control their sexual activities; and, on the other hand, they are given contraceptive devices which seem to indi-

2. op. cit. See pp. 71, 72.
3. *Les cahiers du CTNERHI*, no. 23, Paris.

cate permission, if not encouragement, to freer sexual expression.[4]

It is terribly important to interpret the sexual and violent acts of handicapped people in an institution. What exactly is the person saying or wanting when he or she seeks a sexual relationship in such a place? The person knows that these acts are not 'inoffensive' and 'neutral'. They provoke all sorts of strong reactions from the staff, and sometimes even conflict between staff members. Certainly the person may be governed by a sexual urge, but he or she can also take delight in the strong reactions and conflicts which he or she has provoked.

In the same way, it is important to understand what a Down's syndrome lady of twenty-one is really trying to say when she declares that she wants to go to bed with a man, especially if she is terribly unhappy in her family. No serious psychologist who has any real contact with human beings can say that sexual desire is simply an urge which must be satisfied. We mentioned earlier three situations which illustrate the complexity of apparently sexual behaviour:[5] Edith, who uses her charm to attract men: Micheline, who has captivated Bernard: and Francis, who is influenced by the image his mother has of him. It seems that in none of these situations are the people really looking for sexual pleasure as such, and certainly not for real relationships. Edith

---

4. The authors add that, if one wants to give a complete picture of the problems concerning sexuality and the affectivity of handicapped people in institutions, one has to mention the way they are used frequently to gratify the needs of the staff. This exploitation finds two expressions:

    – the traditional way, which is clandestine, brutal and violent, is rarely punished by institutional authorities and never publicized. It is more frequent than we are led to believe and is especially prevalent in the large 'traditional' institutions.

    – the 'modern' way in more *avant-garde* institutions through the expression of a totally permissive ideology, and even under the pretext of 'healing through love'. The exercise of genital sexuality is practised in a quasi-open manner; it is vulgarized and accompanied not by violence, but by seduction which comes as much from the handicapped person as from the staff. This seems less barbaric than the former way, but it is equally to be condemned. In fact, each time a staff member, in the name of therapy, satisfies his or her own sexual needs he uses the handicapped person as an object, and commits an 'institutional violence'.

5. See chapter 3, p. 64.

is seeking the pleasure of being noticed and of making men jealous of her; Micheline, the pleasure of having Bernard on a leash, giving her a sense of power; and Francis, the pleasure of living up to his mother's image of him.

There are young people who use drugs in a desire to disgrace their fathers. In an underhand way, they are seeking revenge for their father's lack of love, of attention and tenderness. We cannot deny the variety of underlying motivations in behaviour.

Jeremy is a big, gentle lad who suffers from a psychosis. He has great difficulties with language and relationships. He is attracted to the young girls who visit the community and to the beauty of their bodies. Gently, he approaches them to touch them. There is something beautiful in this attraction, but, on the other hand, Jeremy cannot respond to the deep needs of these young girls. Neither can he understand their call for friendship nor their fear of him. He is incapable of being a support to them, or of feeling responsible for them. This attraction will not help him to develop true friendship, where the boundaries are clear and differences are respected. To permit or encourage Jeremy in a physical union with a woman would be to encourage him to a union which is only 'fusional'. It would not help him to become more deeply human.

The role of the educator, primarily, is to help those with a handicap to live humanly and to have sexual relationships only when they can really be human and not divorced from their lives and most fundamental and personal needs. His or her role is to help someone with a mental handicap not simply to express each violent or sexual urge, but to integrate these instincts in a true and permanent relationship.

My experience shows that the sexual drive is more often a cry for relationship than a cry for pleasure. Often it erupts when someone feels alone and anguished. It then seeks expression on the level of genital sexuality. But more deeply, the person is crying out for friendship. However, at the same time the person can be terribly frightened of relationship. We yearn to be loved, but we are very frightened of it because it makes us vulnerable. Sometimes it is easier for a girl to believe that her body is desirable than to believe her person is lovable. Many people with a mental handicap do not believe either in the beauty of their person or in their capacity to love profoundly and to be loved. They are judged so frequently on purely exterior criteria of normality and abnormality; how can they believe that their person is lovable and that they are important just as they are? To reduce genital sexuality to being only a liberation of a passing external urge without attaching it to life and fecundity is to diminish the person.

It is important to interpret acts of genital sexuality in order to understand the most profound needs of the person and to help each one to move towards fulfilment.

INTEGRATION OF SEXUALITY

At l'Arche, it is evident to us that the most essential thing for human beings is to have deep relationships of friendship. In *L'Ange et La Bête*,[6] the authors show a discrepancy between the vision of some parents and that of certain educators. Parents feel their children seek affection above all, while educators think that they search primarily for sexual pleasure.

It seems to me that we must go beyond these two attitudes. Of course, expressions of 'love' on the part of those having a mental handicap are often very affectionate. But, in my opinion, what they seek is much more than a passing emotion or a feeling of affection. They want to be linked to people, entering into a true friendship which involves fidelity. The signs of 'innocent' affection or of 'genital sexuality' are two aspects of the same call, the same cry: 'Do you truly love me and respect me? Do you truly wish to commit yourself to me? Is there really a meaning to my life? Do I really have a place in your heart and in the human community?' So many will receive no answer to these questions. They will continue to cry and never discover their true inner selves. They will continue to provoke their parents and teachers, or simply yield to their wishes.

The goal of education is to help people grow toward wholeness and to discover their place, and eventually exercise their gifts, in a network of friendship and, ideally, in an acknowledged convenant relationship. This means the integration of one's sexuality in a vision of fellowship and friendship. It implies that each one, man or woman, in his or her sexual being, must learn to love others, entering into relationships of communion, gift,

6. *Les cahiers du CTNERHI*, no. 23, Paris.

tenderness and service, using their genital sexuality only in that particular covenant which is blessed by God. The integration of sexuality means that one is no longer ruled by sexual compulsions and the selfish search for pleasure. Rather, it is a matter of being faithful to a covenant with another person.

Such an integration of sexuality is not easy. Sexual urges and desires are strong and can drive a person to intercourse without first passing through the different stages of friendship and communion. So-called 'love' can be seductive and manipulative. It can use others as objects and it can be a way to wield power over others. Sexual urges can also be destructive and they are often linked to aggression and violence.

Nevertheless, in the same sexual urge, there is something very beautiful. There is a deep attraction towards another and a desire for intimacy with the person. There is also the desire to give life to a child. It is important to understand the sexual instinct in its complexity, and in some way to dialogue with it. It cannot be smothered or mastered by will power. It must be integrated, little by little, into a true friendship with another and expressed only in the precise conditions of a covenant blessed by God.

For me, the integration of genital sexuality is different from the sublimation of the sexual instincts of which the followers of Freud speak so often. Sublimation is seen as the orientation of sexual energies into other creative, intellectual or artistic activities. In this a person's pleasure remains the main concern while the importance of relationship with others is neglected. The integration of sexuality, on the other hand, is assumed in a work of love and communion where one seeks the good of another or others, always in a relationship with people as *persons*. The life-giving, vital energy – through gestures of goodness, truth, service and tenderness – is gratified by the loving responses that these gestures call forth.

A TRUE COMMUNITY

In reality, we cannot dissociate the sexual urge from the attraction of love. The folly of the sexual urge is in some sense linked to the folly of love, with its search for intimacy, tenderness and true communion. The important thing is to move not towards fantasies and illusions of intimacy, but towards a true love expressed in communion and gift, and founded on a covenant of commitment. This, in fact, is one of the goals of community. Community is a place of healing and therapy, a place of growth and education: it is also a family where each one can live authentic and liberating relationships.

The first priority is to help those with a mental handicap discover that they are loved with tenderness and care, experienced through the body and in the totality of their being. For this, someone must take the place of a parent; thus is born, little by little, a sense of being part of a new family. Then each one will grow to the discovery that they too are capable of loving, of working, of serving, of living with others as sisters and brothers. In discovering their humanity, they discover the harmony of giving and receiving. But each discovers also that he or she is a child of God, capable of knowing the Lord of the universe who is also Father. Gradually, each one accepts the relativity of his or her handicap and that the most important thing is the heart, that which is capable of loving and serving in openness to God and to others. There is less fear of meeting the world because of the links of friendship, and the sense of belonging to something greater than one's family and one's community. Each one is a person who belongs to all humanity, to the Church and to God, finding the deepest meaning of life in living for others.

A community will only be able to fulfil this role if it is truly community, and not just a group of individuals living in their own way, without any sense of a common bond between them. True community is a place of covenant; like a family, its members are linked to one another in mutual trust and respect, and by a deep sense of belonging. This is expressed in the spontaneity and animation of real celebrations and festivities. A family has one soul and one heart. A collection of individuals has neither heart nor soul; it only has rules and a hierarchy of power; in such a situation people look elsewhere for a life of tenderness and bonds of love. And one of the ways of seeking elsewhere is the cry for genital sexuality, through seduction, obsessions and even perversions.

Community implies a real fellowship where people truly listen to one another in love. In communities like l'Arche, we must try to break down whatever separates those with a handicap from those who come to live with them. Sometimes these walls of separation serve to protect assistants from losing their power. Such walls can only be knocked down by love and mutual trust, where the assistants begin to enter into communion with the person who has a handicap. Assistants come to serve and to give, but also to receive and to discover their own humanity. Slowly, they can accept the risk of loving, knowing how to make gestures of tenderness and affection in a way that will not awaken genital sexuality, but rather bring fulfilment and peace, and awaken the heart because they are a sign of communion and of covenant.

It is important that this communion be liberating, and not stifling. Affectivity and bonds at the level of the heart are very beautiful realities, but they have their dangers. What often happens in a family can also happen in a community. There can be assistants who, instead of liberating those for whom they are responsible, become possessive and use them to satisfy their own emotional needs. They are afraid of loneliness and of separation, and of the aggression that these can imply. They use emotional bonds unconsciously to block growth. In communities like those of l'Arche, it is vitally important to guard against this danger.

Only when the bonds of the heart are liberating and not possessive can the community become a place of celebration and vitality, where suffering can be shared and where each one gives life to the other, discovering their unique call and identity.

If we could stop looking at the manifestations of genital sexuality as a right to pleasure or a problem to be solved, and could recognize it more as a cry to create permanent bonds in order to escape isolation, we would take an enormous step towards understanding true education.

THE IDEAL COMMUNITY?

Yet, even communities which begin joyfully, in a network of freely offered personal relationships, can become closed in on themselves. This is the history of so many communities which began in the mystery of communion and ended in rules and administration. No community is protected from such danger.

True sexual integration, in the way I have described it, needs a community with a heart and a soul, a sense of belonging and celebration, a fruitfulness, but especially many personal relationships. These conditions can never be guaranteed. Hearts can lose confidence and enthusiasm; barriers can grow up between people.

Occasionally I have seen in some communities of l'Arche, signs of lively animation, but closer investigation reveals that those with a mental handicap actually live in isolation, without either the warmth of real friendship and care or the challenge to growth through personal projects. In sickness they do not experience a special tenderness which is so essential at such times. In situations like this, violence erupts, and the desire for genital sexuality is manifested. These are cries for more attention and love. These same cries are heard whenever a community becomes too autocratic, and those with a mental handicap do not share enough in the decisions which affect their lives. In brief, violence and the hunger for genital sexuality arise whenever people with a mental handicap do not feel truly at home.

6

The Celibate Living in Community

THE SUFFERING OF THE CELIBATE

Despite all the human riches one can find in a true community life, it will never totally fill the human heart of a person who lives in celibacy. There will always be a suffering which comes from the absence of a more total intimacy with another and from renouncing physical paternity or maternity. This is true even when one has a privileged friendship with a particular person. One renounces this more total intimacy because one is aware of not being able to live fully and in all truth the demands which are necessarily involved in the total gift of one person to another. One renounces this in order to be faithful to the desire of God.

But marriage also carries its sufferings. The union is never fully satisfying; it can never be a total union because of the simple fact that the two spouses are always in some sense separate. They are never able to enter certain secret areas of the other; there is never perfect clarity between them, partly because of the fears and egoism which still exist in the heart of each one.

Here we touch the deep mystery of the human heart, its vulnerability and its thirst for love and presence, its thirst for infinity. The human being is constantly straining towards this infinity: a thirst to be filled, to be recognized in one's uniqueness, a thirst to be free, to be loving, to be a source of life for others. But this pull towards infinity is lived by a fragile being, a being easily seduced by lies or caught up in fears, capable of hate, and seeking power and admiration in what is only illusion. Our thirst is infinite but it is carried in fragile vessels.

The human heart seems so linked to the sexual organs; and the quest for love is equally linked with the desire to give life. Love, linked in this way to genital sexuality, appears to be the great mystery of the human being. In reality, it is like a marvel-

lous fruit hanging from the tree of life. However, fruit without a
tree is an illusion. Love requires inner strength, order and a
deep rootedness in the person. It implies that the person is
capable of giving to another and, with him or her, of giving to
others. It implies faithfulness to the bonds that have been given,
especially when a relationship is threatened by moments of
difficulty, or when illusion and weakness are exposed.

The thirst for union and fecundity, fruitfulness, in the depths
of the human person is in the image of God himself, who is
absolute love and infinite fecundity. It is therefore holy, and in
order for union and fecundity to be realized in their deepest
harmony, the union must receive power and strength from God
and be marked by the divine qualities of fidelity and truth. This
sacred element in man and woman which draws them to the
triune God can be totally degraded when used only for the
pursuit of pleasure for self, without any recognition of the value
of either fecundity or permanent commitment. Aristotle said that
the worst thing is the corruption of the best thing. This is what
happens when one loves 'without love', without truly wanting
to give oneself to another.

The bonds of love which can exist between a man and a
woman are a mystery. The Song of Songs tells of the fire and
intimacy of love, a sign of the love of God. The poems of St John
of the Cross are songs of love – a passionate love – for the
Beloved. Jesus came not to establish reasonable laws which must
be obeyed in order that human beings and society function well,
but rather to light the fire of the Holy Spirit, to communicate a
passion of love which is reflected also in inner light and an
outpouring of service. Now this fire of the Holy Spirit is given,
not to the wise and the powerful, but to the weak and the
smallest ones, to the poor, to the gentle, to the pure of heart and
the persecuted. To these Jesus shows himself as the Spouse.

There will always be discontent in the human heart; it will
never be able to live wholly in the land of ecstasy and fulfilment.
These are experiences given for a moment but which cannot be
permanently contained in the vulnerability of our hearts. Even
the most beautiful love ends in separation, for death is written
into the human body. In order to welcome that death, or rather,
in order to live love fully in mortal bodies, we must have trust:
life and love are stronger than death; in spite of separation an

invisible union remains, a union which finds its consummation after death, when our mortal bodies will be raised up in glory.

True love is achieved only through suffering and sacrifice, because it is a gift. When we love someone, the well-being, liberty, growth, desires or happiness of this person are more precious than the joy of being with him or her. True love is not possessive, but always liberates. A possessive love stifles and may finally destroy the person. Jesus said that there is no greater love than to give one's life for one's friends. Love is consummated in sacrifice: to give all, we must give our life.

Thus, although the suffering of the celibate is real, it can be lived in hope, a hope which, in a way, assuages the anguish of loneliness. This suffering is nothing in comparison to the suffering of those who, in the exercise of genital sexuality without responsibility, commitment, or fecundity, hope to find a taste of the eternal. Inevitably, they are disappointed, for they find themselves in an even greater isolation: pleasure is so ephemeral and anguish so near!

Many human beings are obliged to live as celibates. Throughout the history of humanity, many men and women have not been able to find the beloved of their hearts. They have lived alone, painfully asking themselves if it is because they are unlovable. For others, the beloved was suddenly torn from them by death. Others entered into the bonds of marriage with the enthusiasm of passionate love, but without the human means for living and deepening the relationship, which eventually broke down. Then, there are all those who carried severe handicaps in their flesh or their spirit. Perhaps they had a fear of relationship, or they had violent or depressive characters. Some had bodies which were mutilated, and others were unable to live a harmonious relationship with another. Many were rejected and devalued. For so many different reasons, they were unable to live a union of love in their flesh. Yet, our experience shows us that when such people live not alone but in community, or in a network of friendship, strengthened and healed by a love which comes from God, it is possible for them to find fulfilment in a life of celibacy.

IN THE ABSENCE OF COMMUNITY

The tragedy is when there is no fraternal community. When human beings live isolated in collectivities without a soul, how can they ever learn to integrate their sexuality, especially in a society which, through its mass media, continually emphasizes sexual needs and at the same time banalizes sexual relationships, failing to demonstrate what is sacred in a true covenant?

We need continually to be reminded of the sacred aspect of genital sexuality. God reveals himself to man in his heart and in his deep emotional life. If we vulgarize genital sexuality and the emotional life, we deny the sacred value of the human heart; we risk destroying it; and in so doing, we destroy the house, the temple, which was made to welcome the gift of God. This is serious. We cannot destroy God, but we can destroy people who are capable of receiving him.

Sometimes people say that the Church and religious leaders have no right to speak of genital sexuality because many of them are celibates. Experience shows me that priests often have a great understanding of the human heart through the thousands and thousands of confidences given to them in individual confessions or through spiritual direction. Many of them have more knowledge of the demands and difficulties of love than psychologists. They have received these confidences in a deeper light than psychology, in the light of the intimate and spiritual consciences of people.

The Church is right in announcing the sacred aspect of the genital sexual life. But it is necessary for us, the grassroots Christians, to know how to create communities. For, without community, without true love, without forgiveness, without covenant, without celebration, it is not possible to integrate genital sexuality in authentic human relationships. One risks becoming the prey of one's own sexual urges or those of others, the prey of all kinds of seductions, or else one hides behind thick walls, frightened of relationships.

This is why in our epoch it is necessary to work at all costs to create true communities which welcome isolated and distressed people. It is they who have the greatest need to live in a network of friendship where they will really find their place and where they will be valued.

THE NEED FOR MODELS

For people with a mental handicap to live their celibacy positively and with serenity, it is necessary for them to know men and women living in the same community who have truly welcomed celibacy with peace as a gift from God. If they only see educators who begrudge their celibacy, they will have more difficulty in assuming their own celibacy. Married assistants, through their love, can give stability to those with a mental handicap. The peace and warmth of their family life can be a source of deep healing for their hearts. But they cannot be real models for those who cannot marry.

If celibacy is difficult for those with a mental handicap, it is equally difficult for assistants. Many come to l'Arche searching, like so many of the young of our times. They are often fragile in their emotional development; they also sincerely want to be committed to the struggle for a better world. This fragility and a certain idealism often go together. But the experience of living with those having a mental handicap, in a community inspired by a Christian faith, touches their own hearts. Their inner selves are strengthened and they discover solid motivations for the direction of their lives. Their hearts are awakened in the relationship with someone with a mental handicap, whose poverty, child-like confidence and cry to be loved are like an invitation, a call, to enter into a covenant relationship involving the gift of their life in fidelity.

Many assistants come to l'Arche attracted by our community life, inspired by the Beatitudes and by the relationship with the person having a mental handicap. The beginnings are often life-giving. The assistants discover real fraternity; their hearts are touched; many of their capacities are revealed which until then had been hidden. Later they seem to reach their own limits and the limits of the community. This is the moment of truth! Often at this time, assistants begin to discover the dimension of prayer. They discover in their own depths the presence of God and a call to live with Jesus in the poor; a profound change is wrought by this experience of faith. They discover that the commitment to the poor cannot be lived without Jesus, prayer, the nourishment of the Word of God and the body of Christ. Throughout this period of discovery they need to be supported in truth by a priest or minister or another man or woman of God.

A short while ago, a young assistant in one of our l'Arche communities came to see me. She spoke to me of her journey in community. This young woman is competent and deeply present to those in her home. But she herself is fragile at the level of her emotional life. She lives close to anguish, having suffered much in her childhood. She has known intimate relationships with a number of men during her life. She is so afraid of being alone, and afraid of her own emptiness. She has a desperate need to be listened to and to be loved. Her work with and her presence to those who have a handicap have nourished her and helped her to structure herself, but not sufficiently to bring her emotional life to maturity. At the same time, she is aware that her pursuit of men lacks authenticity and that she is using her sexuality to attract men to her in order to fill her own emptiness and to escape from loneliness. Her anguish and her call for affection impedes her growth, keeps her from finding her inner strength and from achieving true inner liberty and autonomy. She told me that she felt the need to put an end to these affectionate, but immature relationships in order to grow further. It is evident that her meeting with Jesus and her life of prayer have helped her to be freer *vis-à-vis* her psychological tendencies and her hunger to be loved.

Essentially this young woman, product of a broken family, is typical of so many other young people and so many of those with a mental handicap. The depths of her being must be strengthened through prayer, through the challenges and joys of community life, through coming into contact with the poor and serving them. She must struggle with her psychological desires in order to grow into a real and more generous love. And then, one day, she will be able to see clearly and respond to God's call to marriage or to celibacy.

The tragedy of the young is their emotional fragility. Their hearts are rich in the capacity to love. They are intuitive; they see clearly the dangers and the hypocrisies of our world and of so many of the political movements and social organizations. They desire to live authentic lives. They wish to be committed, but where and how? They feel so vulnerable and powerless in front of the forces which shape society and the world. They need examples to encourage and strengthen them. They need those who, by the witness of their lives, invite others to a permanent commitment. Often they cannot find such models. Confronted with the gap between their fragility and their ideals, they fall into discouragement and often despair. Some of them come to l'Arche seeking a refuge or even an escape into the spiritual world. Some will need psychological support, in order to find the stability necessary for growth.

All those who find hope in l'Arche must pass through certain stages, and sometimes through difficult stages, before they can truly put down their roots in the community. The crucial question for many of them is celibacy. Is it possible? Their own emotional needs are so deep!

Some assistants find their fulfilment through marriage and others discover celibacy, not as an indeterminate period of waiting, but rather as a gift of God. This discovery may take long years of maturation before they can live celibacy in response to a deep call from God. Then they can say 'yes' with as much joy and enthusiasm as those who marry. They discover that it is much easier when they have made this decision clearly, relying on the faithfulness and love of God, than when they were still in a state of indecision. This welcome of celibacy as a response to a call of God, and a call of the poor, implies that they have spoken with a priest or a man or woman of God who has confirmed them in this choice. It also implies that they have decided to dedicate their capacities for human love to God alone, who is hidden in the hearts of the poor. The decision to say 'yes' does not mean a hardened heart or an escape from relationships into the spiritual or into activities of service.

On the contrary, it is made so that one may live more fully a covenant with the poor. When the heart is open to Jesus as a friend and spouse, we become more sensitive to human sufferings, closer to others, more welcoming and more loving towards them. However, once we have welcomed this gift of celibacy, that does not mean there is no more suffering or questions, for in this area of the emotional life, the heart always remains vulnerable. At l'Arche, our life leads us to lower the walls around our hearts so that we may be open to the tenderness of relationships. We do not hide our hearts or protect them. This willingness to be vulnerable brings a great richness to relationships, but it can also create insecurity and a fear of being hurt. We are only able to live this insecurity if the heart is rooted in Jesus and in the poor, and if we seek, in the Eucharist and prayer, an encounter with the One who loves us and calls us by name to fidelity to those with whom we are bonded. The suffering of a celibate can become, at this point, a sign of his or her love. It is a gift and an offering of the whole self to Jesus and to his friends.

What is specific, however, in l'Arche is that the celibacy of assistants springs frequently from their covenant with those who have a mental handicap. Many of the latter cannot get married; their celibacy is enforced. The call of Jesus to celibacy for some assistants is thus linked to this covenant with those in distress and in pain. Their celibacy springs from the love that binds them together in the heart of God.

MY OWN EXPERIENCE OF VULNERABILITY

My personal experience shows me clearly my need of community and my need of prayer if I am to live celibacy. When I am in my community with those whom I love and who love me, I am completely at peace. I experience an inner wholeness. I am able to love with my heart, confident that it will be received without the risk of division or turmoil. In personal encounters, there is often a very great peace, a depth of silence, which is, I believe a sign of the presence of God. In these moments my heart is still vulnerable, but at the same time, I sense a strength and unity within me.

On the other hand, when I am travelling alone, far from the community, and if I do not remain in prayer and in contact with my own centre and the presence of Jesus, I experience a sense of tremendous vulnerability and fragility. I have the feeling of being tossed about by all kinds of winds, attracted by any kind of seduction. Sometimes I have the impression of having neither the strength of will nor the virtue to protect myself. In these moments, I try to entrust myself to God. I pray that he will protect me and keep me from all harm. But I experience a very great poverty.

When I reflect on these moments of poverty, two things become clear. Firstly, I realize that in the intensity of community life I have learned to let my barriers fall, which allows me to be myself. In this way I have learned to live with my vulnerability in order to welcome the other and to show that I truly love him or her.

When I was a naval officer, I had the impression of having more 'virtue' and more 'will', but I was not vulnerable. I had hidden myself behind a façade of strength. Living in community, we learn not to hide any longer; barriers are not necessary because we have confidence in one another. Thus, when we leave the community, we feel exposed in our vulnerability, especially when our hearts no longer feel protected by an inner peace coming from the presence of God. This confirms me in the knowledge that, even if sometimes I must travel and experience my vulnerability in its nakedness, my life is meant to be lived in community. I need the community in order to live on a certain level of truth and inner liberty. Without it I am too close to anguish and have not enough security. I feel far from those who are strong, virtuous, and self-willed. I feel at home with weak and vulnerable people, like myself.

Secondly, I have discovered that the anguish I experience when I am alone, isolated, and vulnerable is favourable ground for the forces of evil. In some way I sense the meaning of the words of St John on the subject of Judas: 'Satan entered into him.' Sometimes the anguish so impoverishes me that I realize that, without God's protection, Satan would provoke me to do the most foolish things. This experience of my poverty and the darkness within me could discourage me; in reality, it does not, but it calls me to live community more fully, and to grow in truth and trust in God.

CELIBACY AND THE MYSTERY OF LOVE

But, as we have said, community life with its celebrations and its sense of sharing is not enough. Someone with a mental handicap needs a unique and personal relationship. I am deeply moved by the sensitivity of heart in some men and women with a mental handicap that I have known. There is David who deeply loves Rachael, a young assistant who left to live in a developing country. Time and again, he sends her part of his salary 'for the handicapped children in her centre there'. He says: 'Rachael is my friend; it is because of her that I work.' I sense the power and delicacy of the love in his heart as something sacred and divine. This is not a dream, for this love has truly helped him to find a profound balance. It is his secret, and it must be respected.

There is a similar secret in the heart of Richard. He is not a very religious man. He believes, but rarely goes to Mass or to evening prayer. One day, whispering in my ear, he asked me to go with him to the chapel to pray. There he said a prayer of consecration to the Blessed Virgin Mary, putting himself totally in her hands. I was deeply touched by this gesture.

Laurence, too, never goes to Mass except for funerals and weddings. This is not because he has anything against the Mass; he is simply not in the habit of going. However, he was very touched by the story of Our Lady of La Salette, the apparition of Mary to two children who saw her weeping. 'She was like a mother beaten by her children and driven from her home,' one of the children said after the apparition. When I welcomed Laurence to l'Arche, he, too, had wept many tears. There was a kind of complicity between him and that woman who had wept on the mountain. It is the secret of his heart.

Many men and women I know in l'Arche have a secret in the depths of their hearts, a secret through which they are linked with someone of the other sex. Whether this person plays the role of father or mother, of big brother or big sister for them is not important. What is important is that they love.

I am shocked when I see some people ridiculing the bonds of love which unite a handicapped man with a handicapped woman. Often these are bonds of a secret and sacred tenderness which must be respected. Perhaps they are called to live these bonds only on the level of the heart, in the simplicity of love. It should not be assumed that these bonds must necessarily become physical and sexual as such.

Each human being has a secret love which he or she is able to realize either in marriage or in the joy and happiness of community life. It is this secret which gives us life and inspiration. The absence of such a secret or, perhaps worse, the stifling or betrayal of the secret, brings death and leads to despair.

The heart is so beautiful, so innocent ... but it can be betrayed, scorned, broken. I remember Laurence, a man about twenty-five years old, who was marked by a very unhappy past. Strictly speaking, his handicap could be said to be mild, but having been put in an institution at a very early age, he had a terribly wounded heart. His mother had abandoned her home when he was still a very small child. His father, whom he loved very much and who had brought him up, had to be admitted to a psychiatric hospital. This was the time when Laurence himself was placed in an institution. He was full of anger and violence. Even if he found l'Arche better than the institution, he was not really happy with us. At table he would often explode. One day he met Christine, a young woman with a slight mental handicap, but very worried emotionally. She seduced him. In approaching him with tenderness, she awakened his heart. It was astonishing to see in the space of a few months, the change which took place in him. He became more gentle, more calm; his face became peaceful and relaxed; at table, he would listen to others; all his aggression seemed to have melted away.

In obtaining information about Christine who lived in another centre, the team discovered that she was a dangerous woman. She attracted men in order to control them and get them to give her money and gifts, and then she would drop them for another. The team did not know what to do. Finally, they decided to let events run their course and they prepared themselves to carry and support Laurence when she dropped him. That is what happened, and Laurence fell into depression: he closed in on himself again, even more than before. This experience confirmed his fear of women. But, it was amazing to have seen the beauty of his heart. Loved in his being as a man, he had been transformed, although, unhappily, only for a time. Love is the most beautiful reality, but a reality which can also be very dangerous if it is not founded on a true commitment.

The sexual life, if it is not lived in a covenant given by God, can obscure the heart, render it opaque. Sexuality can be a sacrament of relationship, but it also can be the death of relationship. The kiss can obstruct the word, that word which is absolutely necessary to deepen the relationship. The sexual instinct is so powerful that it can carry a couple to physical union without going through the stages of friendship and sharing needed in order to know each other. Such a union has no solid foundation on which the future can be built.

THE MYSTERY OF LOVE WITH JESUS

The more I advance in age, and perhaps in wisdom, as I listen to those who have suffered and those who are growing in freedom, the more I am confirmed in my faith in Jesus Christ. I see with more and more clarity that the greatest human suffering is isolation, turning in on oneself, and the lack of love. In discovering their darkness and anguish, some people are engulfed in sadness. Others react and develop a super-ego; their anguish becomes an energy driving them to success and domination, and they become aggressive and always want to be noticed. Others seek compensations in violence, alcohol, or drugs; they try to forget and to run away from their darkness. They seek frantically to fill up their inner emptiness.

Who can help us human beings to welcome our own fragility, which is hidden behind the barriers of our fears? Who can help us to assume the flaws of our history and our being, our agonies and weaknesses, even our mortality? We are so very poor: humanly, psychically, morally and spiritually, and we are all bound in that radical poverty: death. We all carry within us a depth of guilt.

Can humanity be saved? Or is it rather condemned to compromise, to untruth and to war? Neither science nor technology is able to save humanity. They do not have the means to liberate hearts, opening them to love and sharing. Psychoanalysis is able to free certain blockages, but it cannot change a heart of stone into a heart of love; it is not able to give life, hope and a taste for sharing. War and violence cannot bring peace: they engender hate and vengeance. And salvation cannot come through politics, because a change of structures touches only the exterior; it is our egotistic human hearts which must be transformed.

I believe that God alone can change the interior of our hearts, through the revelation that we are loved, and lovable, that we are of value, and loved by God, just as we are, with all our resistance and our darkness as well as with all our gifts. There is no need to be perfect; we are, each one of us God's beloved children. Thus, in loving us, God gives us life and the strength to grow ever deeper in love towards a new wholeness.

The Father so loved humans in their poverty and their wounds that he sent his Son, the Word, to reveal his love. He sent Jesus, born of the woman, Mary, to announce to all men and women that each one is loved, that no one need be alone or lost. This is the good news: the answer to our anguish and isolation. With him and in him, it is possible to live just as we are, to welcome our handicaps, our deficiencies, our wounds; even to accept our mortality and to have hope.

Jesus is the intermediary *par excellence*, who has said to each of us: 'Fear not, I love you; you have value in my eyes; you are able to live; come, advance along the road of life to become, in your turn, an intermediary who will reveal to others that they are forgiven and loved.' Jesus is there, present in the heart of each one of us, but we often are afraid of him, and so we continue to run away or hide behind noise and all sorts of commotion. We refuse to enter into our inner selves to listen to him, the Silent Lover, hidden in the centre of our being. We find it hard to believe that he is hidden in the vulnerability of our hearts, deeper than the anguish and the fear, far deeper than the walls we have built around this vulnerability and the wounds within us.

When we discover that we are loved with an eternal love, with a love beyond all time and space, which goes even beyond death, then everything begins to change, all becomes possible, all can be accepted and loved.

The healing of a person comes, above all, through a personal union with Jesus who has revealed that he is the Friend and the Beloved who touches, awakens and fills the heart.

It is true that the revelation of the love of God almost always comes through a relationship with someone, and in the heart of a community. But the community can never reach and touch a person in a total way; only a person can touch deeply another person. In a community, there is not the covenant of one person with another as in marriage or in the parent–child relationship. The covenant of community, profound as it is, can never guarantee that a certain person will always stay physically close to another. It guarantees only that there will always be someone there, inspired by the same spirit. In order for the human heart to find its roots in a covenant relationship, it must find Jesus. Someone having a mental handicap, who is sometimes so limited and whose heart is so full of suffering, has a greater need than anyone else to encounter Jesus and hear the Good News of love. There is so little possibility of choosing marriage. Such a person experiences a deep poverty. He or she is unable to fend totally for him or herself, and is in need of others, but above all, in need of Jesus. The Good News permits those who are wounded to discover their deepest identity and vocation, and permits them to discover their place in the community and in the Church.

Society gives the first places to the rich and powerful, to those who are productive and useful. In this system, those with a mental handicap are always in the last place, if they have a place at all, for often they will not even have that. Frequently they are killed by the inhumanity or ignorance of humans at the moment of their birth if not before, or they are totally cast aside as they begin to grow up. And if they are given even that last place, it is given grudgingly because it is expensive for society.

The Gospel is announced to the poor. The poor are at the heart of the new structure; the first place belongs to them, theirs is the Good News of the presence of Jesus, the Good News which is rejected, most of the time, by the rich and the busy who are satisfied with themselves.

Celibacy remains a mystery. It is found as a vocation in many religions, even in the religion of ancient Rome; thus it has been shown as a special way of uniting oneself with God and preparing oneself to receive a new and more intimate union with him. Jesus spoke about it very discreetly when he said: 'There are eunuchs who have made themselves that way for the sake of the kingdom of heaven. Let anyone accept this who can' (Matthew 19:12).

Celibacy for the sake of the Kingdom, answering the call of Jesus, has always been lived in the Church by those who were able to welcome it and to choose it. I believe that Jesus wishes to come in a special way to the aid of those who have no choice in their celibacy. He wants to touch them in the depths of their hearts, bringing them the peace of a new love. It is true that the Good News is announced to the poor, but it is essential that they have a milieu where they are able to receive and live this Good News. It is important that someone with a mental handicap comes to know that celibacy can be welcomed as a gift of God through which the heart will be fulfilled.

This is not to say that all this takes place without suffering. It takes time to heal the heart, to knock down the barriers, to find the balance in relationships. Some people never fully achieve this, engulfed as they are in anguish and violence. Sometimes they even have to leave the community or they ask to leave. For others, the challenge demands much effort, and growth takes many years with moments of progress and moments of failure, during which they need much support and friendship. Their hearts always seem to remain vulnerable. Some, however, seem truly to discover Jesus, the beloved of their hearts. They live at certain moments an authentic experience of the love of God, their hearts burning with that love.

Personally, I am astonished to see, in my own community where the workshops and so many of the homes are mixed, how much peace there is in this area of sexuality. The way of life, the dynamism of community life, the quality of the assistants and the spiritual life all contribute to this peace. Of course, there are sufferings, disturbances, ambiguities, but in general those with a mental handicap seem to enjoy a liberty of heart that few other people in the world attain.

My experience, and the confidences which I have received through the years, show me that the priest or spiritual guide plays an important role in this calming of the heart, in the growth in love, in the acceptance of one's handicap and in the hope of being able to overcome it realistically. The priest as confidant, as a spiritual father and as the presence of Jesus in the sacrament of reconcilation, becomes a support and a privileged companion. But many people, even priests, are ignorant of the role which they have concerning the integration of genital sexuality and the growth of love, not only for the person with a handicap but for all believers; and in addition, they fail to see their role in calling others to live celibacy as a sign of the Kingdom and a personal meeting place with Jesus.

THE ASSISTANTS AND THE MYSTERY OF LOVE

Much that has been said about those with a mental handicap, can also be said about the assistants. Their hearts, too, are thirsty for a special love with someone. And, like the young woman of whom we spoke earlier, they have their struggles. They must learn to fix their priorities. They must know what they want and say 'yes' to growth, to the efforts and struggles it implies; they must find help to remain faithful in times of trial or temptation; they must discover the meaning of covenant.

Sometimes, God unites a man and a woman in a special love, not to lead them to marriage, but to strengthen them in celibacy as a gift of God. In these bonds, the woman's heart is awakened and protected by the man just as the man's heart is awakened and protected by the woman. This special relationship, far from distracting them from their vocation, calls them to go even further in their gift to God and to the poor. This love reveals itself to be fruitful. Francis de Sales, bishop of Geneva, wrote to Jeanne de Chantal, who later became the foundress of the Visitation Order, that when he thought of her in prayer it was not a distraction from God, on the contrary, it plunged him even deeper into the Holy Trinity. Similarly, Francis of Assisi had need of Clare and Clare had need of Francis. Mary, the mother of Jesus had need of Joseph and Joseph had need of Mary. They loved each other in the heart of God.

I wonder whether it is not necessary in our days, when celibacy is so questioned, ridiculed and made difficult to live, for people to have a deep experience of friendship and of love with another that springs from the heart of God in order to help them live their celibacy for Jesus and for the poor. Such love is a free gift of God and, like all gifts, it implies sacrifice and renunciation. We so quickly take the gifts of God for granted and consider them as our right. If God gives this love, he wants us to live it in joy and also in abandonment with regard to the future.

One of the difficulties of welcoming and living celibacy in l'Arche is that, strictly speaking, celibacy has no status outside religious life, in which one pronounces vows and makes a solemn profession. There it is clearly a celebration in which the religious community, family and friends rejoice. This public announcement is a support. But for most of the people of l'Arche, the declaration of an enforced celibacy would not have much meaning. Should an assistant announce his or her own celibacy with a celebration, or remain in solidarity with those who have no choice and no status?

In one of our communities in India, a Hindu man with a mild, but real, handicap, announced that he had become a Brahmacharya: in other words, one who renounces the bonds of marriage in order to consecrate all things to God. In general, a Brahmacharya presides over the Puja, the offering of fruits and flowers to God. This decision gave him peace, even if it was his parents who rather pushed him into it. Then he added: 'Anyway, it is better not to be married, because it is difficult to live with a woman!' Nevertheless, he had found a structure for living his celibacy and for announcing it. It was important because, in India, those who are not married are considered inferior.

There is no option like this in Western countries, where there remains a lack of social status for celibates who are not priests or religious, which makes the acceptance of that state more difficult, both for those with a handicap and for the assistants. To the extent that community life shared by celibate men and women is recognized as socially acceptable (and this is not always the case), it may help them to live their celibacy in a more positive way.

All these questions are not resolved and they cannot be, because the welcome of celibacy is very personal, touching the very fragility of one's being at different moments and ages in one's life. But we must ensure the structures, the friendship, the mutual aid, the dynamism, the love in community life and the spirituality which will allow people to live in celibacy in joy.

In the hearts of each one, married or celibate, there are moments of anguish, disturbance, frustration, isolation, sometimes even disequilibrium in the genital sexual life. There are times of fear, of escape, times when one cries out in anguish. Each man and woman must accept this difficult reality. We are not yet in paradise. We hope, for ourselves and for each other, to attain a maximum of peace, of happiness, of love and of balance. But we all await that transition when we are broken and stripped of everything: death. Happiness, if it is in personal and community fulfilment, in the celebration of unity, is also in the waiting, beyond the transition of death, for that gift to come: the wedding feast of Heaven, meeting Jesus face to face and heart to heart.

7

Unity in Marriage

Recently, during our community's Open Day I had the joy of meeting with three couples: six people, four of whom were former members of l'Arche. We talked and laughed together. We remembered the 'good old days'. In my heart, I rejoiced in the authentic harmony and peace which reigned in these couples. I knew each one's story, the story before and the story after the marriage. These stories were marked by suffering and moments of anguish. I remembered ten years earlier, I had gently teased Jean-Paul, one of the men: 'If you don't get your teeth straightened, you'll never get married.' At that time, Jean-Paul was sure that marriage was not for him, so he told me to 'buzz-off'! Some years later, he had straightened his teeth . . . and then . . .

THE BIRTH OF A TRUE RELATIONSHIP

Whether they live together in community or not, there comes a time when a man and a woman having mental handicaps are attracted to each other, even if there are not many verbal exchanges. Perhaps the sufferings of the past, the rejections they have known create a greater solidarity between them. Often they understand each other without words. Little by little, they sense that perhaps they will be able to live together in mutual support and love for each other. They take the step as a couple. Then the question is: how to help them to walk together, to discern the stages and to deepen their relationship in truth.

It is an extraordinary thing for a man with a handicap to discover that he is loved, not only by an assistant, an elder brother or sister, but also by a young woman of his age who is perhaps in the same centre. Something new takes place in his being: he discovers a new dimension of wholeness. Faced with

119

such a development, the educator is called to help both persons to become aware of the beauty of these new bonds of love and, also, the responsibilities which they imply. It is not a question of taking these bonds lightly, whether by the people with a handicap, or by the parents or educators.

WHO DECIDES WHAT?

At l'Arche, as at any other centre, we (like parents) are confronted by the fact that people with a mental handicap are not usually able to cope alone with life on a practical level. Even if there is enough money, they need help signing forms and so on. Others must intervene in their lives in order that they have the fullest human life possible. This means that their emotional life is observed, looked at, analysed, sometimes programmed. This is the tragedy. They need permission and direction. In every way this distorts things. If a person with a mental handicap were able to do what he wanted, things would be simpler and more true. This was the case with Paul and Marie of whom we will speak later. They had been classified as 'mentally deficient' but, in reality, this was not true. They were perfectly capable of managing by themselves, with some slight support. In fact, most of the time, someone with a mental handicap looks around to know what his elders or the educators think. He is dependent on their attention and their support. He does not always have the interior strength to say: 'I am going to do it.'

Thus, it is the people around them who either encourage and support or else forbid the couple who have mental handicaps to move towards marriage.

When, outside of marriage, one encourages someone having a mental handicap to live as a couple and to have sexual relations, it is still the elders who decide. It is they who say: 'This couple can be happy and fully human only if they love and fully profit from the exercise of their sexuality.' But, at the same time, they say: 'Above all, no children.' They even administer contraceptives or, if a child is conceived, they demand an abortion. Thus it was that Emmanuelle, of whom we will speak in chapter 8, had to battle with her educators to keep her child.

The majority of people with a mental handicap are not free. Their mental handicap makes them dependent. It is the responsibility of the team of educators or assistants to lead them into living with the greatest independence possible. Thus it is that at l'Arche, as elsewhere, we take decisions for others which affect their lives. It is true that we encourage some couples to move towards marriage and discourage others. Of the three couples I mentioned earlier, those who were former members of l'Arche had left their home in l'Arche to live more independently. And, it was from this more independent living that they moved towards marriage. I find that more true and more wholesome.

THE BEAUTY AND THE SERIOUSNESS OF SEXUAL RELATIONSHIPS

It is true that at l'Arche we do not want to belittle sexual relationships. We do not believe that they are just a therapeutic means, or a way for someone to express himself. We believe in the beauty, in the gravity and, I would say in the mystery of sexuality as an expression of a profound communion between two persons and the gift of their being to each other, in a reciprocal and permanent commitment.

To affirm such a belief is an enormous challenge in these times when sexuality is so vulgarized by the mass media and when others propose that those with handicaps should be given every help and material means to exercise their right to sexuality and to pleasure. My fear today is that, instead of helping those with handicaps to discover the love of a couple, with all its intimacy and the bond it implies, they are led towards the mirage of easy sexuality without responsibility, without a permanent bond between two people, without true fecundity. This form of sexuality finally leads them to disappointment and a new isolation, because it does not respond to their deepest needs, to their thirst for a covenant relationship. The attraction of man for woman, and of woman for man, can be profound, a thirst for tenderness which nourishes itself through sexuality and which leads to it. But, for that sexuality to be truly human, springing up from relationship and strengthening it, people must have a clear awareness of their identity, knowing who they are and what they wish to make of their lives. It is essential that there be a desire to share one's life in a permanent way with another. Those who exercise their sexuality without having an emotional maturity, without knowing what is actually sought in a sexual relationship, aggravate their state of confusion. Far from developing a sense of identity, it is diminished.

We are touching here the heart of the problem which separates the position of l'Arche from other options. We esteem genital sexuality as a beautiful and powerful reality which calls forth the person in the depths of his or her being. It is a means of exceptional fruitfulness, a unique means of expression: it is not something superficial.

The unique friend – the husband or the wife – is not simply a partner as in a sport. He or she is the beloved, the chosen one of the heart, to whom one entrusts that which is most intimate in one's body and in one's heart. The exercise of sexuality leads to a new relationship. The values of gift and communion implied in the gestures of love carry with them something absolute. This reciprocal gift of one to the other opens them both more deeply to others, to the universe and to God. By this, they become, for each other, not an idol of worship, but an icon, a sign of the presence of God.

In the Christian vision, this mutual gift of the man and the woman, this new bond through the body and genital sexuality, is so profound that it is acknowledged as the image of that which unites Christ with his Church: 'Husbands should love their wives just as Christ loved the Church and sacrificed himself for her ... For this reason, a man must leave his father and mother, and be joined to his wife, and the two will become one body. This mystery has many implications; but I am saying it applies to Christ and the Church' (Ephesians 5:25, 31–32). The most authentic Christian version does not deny, condemn, or devalue genital sexuality; on the contrary, it sees it as a reality so beautiful and so profound that it can be lived fully and most humanly only if the two persons recognize the bonds which unite them forever; these are a covenant, founded on the covenant of each one with God.

IN DAILY LIFE

Genital sexuality is a sign of love and friendship, of gift and communion. Because of this it involves all of life. Sexual relationships are like the summit, a celebration of unity. But this summit means there must be a base, a daily life together, a life in common. And this requires a milieu which is the home.

Through the exercise of genital sexuality, people give themselves to one another in their hearts and in their bodies. The body is the place of intimacy, signifying the intimacy of hearts. The body given by one becomes precious to the other, it is the body of the beloved. In this relationship, which implies and calls forth a covenant, one becomes, in some way, responsible for the body of the other. We become responsible for that which we tame, says the fox in Saint Exupéry's *The Little Prince*. We love the other in his or her body and spirit not only when he or she is healthy, but also when he or she is weak and tired. The love which is contained in the body not only rejoices in the encounter: it also desires to carry the other, to support and help him or her in times of trial; it is service and kindness in daily life. As John Paul II so strongly expresses it:

> . . . sexuality, by means of which man and woman give themselves to one another through the acts which are proper and exclusive to spouses, is by no means something purely biological, but concerns the innermost being of the human person as such. It is realized in a truly human way only if it is an integral part of the love by which a man and woman commit themselves totally to one another until death. The total physical self giving would be a lie if it were not the sign and fruit of a total personal self giving in which the whole person, including the temporal dimension, is present. If the person were to withhold something, or reserve the possibility of deciding otherwise in the future, by this very fact he or she would not be giving totally.[1]

Sexuality lived as covenant serves life: through it the family is built in the service of the little one, the child. It is here that sexuality finds its fullest meaning, that it makes a man and a woman fellow-workers with God to give life to another human person. It is through this that the couple open themselves to a reality which is beyond them: when a man and a woman discover themselves capable of giving life, capable of putting themselves profoundly in the service of a fragile little being, capable of

---

1. Jean Paul II, *Familiaris Consortio: Regarding the Role of the Christian Family in the Modern World*, p. 20. Catholic Truth Society S.357 1981.

becoming parents. This opening frees them from the prison which can make a couple close in on itself.

The sexual relationship, when cut off from daily life, is torn up from its roots and never bears fruit. It is but a moment of excitement, of contact, of pleasure cut off from reality. It does not involve responsibility with regard to the other. It is lived, more or less, like a game; it is not a sign of commitment. It is not the gesture of tenderness and trust between two people linked in a profound way. Thus, in the unconscious, fear persists. The exercise of sexuality risks becoming a tactic of seduction in order to keep the other. If I lose my beauty or dynamism, will you leave me? The exercise of genital sexuality without a recognized and expressed commitment remains terribly fragile, subject to the moods, the fears and the passions of one or the other, and to constant doubt: 'You love me because I please you today, but do you truly love me for myself?'

Clearly, for those with a mental handicap, the risk of isolation when one is abandoned by one's partner does not take the same form as it does for those without a handicap. They are often taken in hand by other people; they are dependent on educators, parents, or tutors. Thus, they will not be alone if the companion with whom they had lived and had sexual relations leaves them for another. Sexual relations do not have the same significance for someone with a handicap, taken into care in a residence or an institution, as they do for a man and a woman who wish to live with another, and for whom sexual relations are part of the sharing of life and a sign of their friendship and commitment.

To facilitate the exercise of genital sexuality in a residence without taking any responsibility for the other person or for running a home and bringing up children, is to debase sexuality, reducing it to the most superficial and exterior level. To do this with a person who has a mental handicap is to devalue him or her.

DIFFICULTIES IN LIVING COVENANT RELATIONSHIPS IN
MARRIAGE

To live an authentic covenant in marriage is not without great difficulties. It is important not to ignore them. Many, in the euphoria of honeymoon and marriage, forget the sorrowful aspect of the covenant. In attaching oneself to one man or one woman, one, in effect, renounces thousands of others. In rooting oneself in one land, one renounces all other lands. In giving oneself to one person, one loses the freedom to give oneself to others. This grief, this loss of liberty are necessary in order to welcome a new liberty, that which we discover in a covenant fully lived, the liberty of marriage, the liberty of paternity and maternity, the liberty of knowing onself to be loved and capable of love.

The beginnings of a deep and intimate relationship between a man and a woman are often full of joy; everything is euphoric. The barriers built around their hearts, which until now held them in isolation, fall down. They are liberated from their fears and their anguish, from all that kept them from expressing themselves. However, after a certain time, clouds begin to appear in the relationship. In the beginning, the light of one called forth the light of the other. Then the light of one touches the darkness of the other, and finally the darkness of one touches the darkness of the other. They get on each others' nerves and become blocked, one to the other. Love risks being transformed into hate.

The transition from the euphoria of encounter to blockages and inability to communicate with each other is very sad. In the early days of marriage, the man leaves his work quickly in order to be with his wife. He speaks freely; he is enthusiastic, attentive, sensitive. Then, little by little, he begins to be more taken up by his work, or some social, political or religious activity. He comes home later and later. He is tired, less enthusiastic. He loses himself in television. Perhaps he begins to drink. The wife gives herself more and more to the children; she also works, and, little by little, a wall grows up between them.

This evolution of the relationship between a husband and wife is well known. It happens frequently these days; so many couples are separating and seeking a divorce. The man and the woman are finding themselves alone, frustrated, angry, depressed, and unable to live in that atmosphere of conflict and aggression. Finally they part. Their hearts are vulnerable. New relationships are regarded with suspicion or distrust. The wound continues in fears and doubts: 'Will I be able to remain faithful? Will the other remain faithful? Was it my fault or the other's? Where did I go wrong?'

The man and the woman did not realize that the point of the blockage could instead have been the point of growth. When that which is negative in one touches that which is negative in the other, they may be able to move to a new level in their relationship and their life together with their children, providing they find help to get through the tunnel, or find new inner resources.

The union of the man and the woman, and the life with their children, are there for the growth and healing of each other. They are there to grow together in love and service, towards a true maturity, to be better able to open themselves to others, to the world and to God. This demands that certain barriers and egotistical and egocentric tendencies, built in childhood, must be broken down. This hurts. That is why there is confusion and suffering when one or the other or both at the same time begin to touch their anguish and their limits. But one must not flee from these moments; one must not, at any cost, run away from the difficulties and the anguish because, not only growth and deepening, but also healing would be impeded.

MARRIAGE

But is a covenant relationship between a man and a woman possible? Is love anything more than an euphoric moment which always ends in blockages and hate? Isn't this the experience of so many couples?

I believe that such a permanent relationship is possible only when the heart of each has been touched by God and healing has begun. It is this encounter with God which permits a couple to face all the demands of the relationship. In the past, and even today in some countries, the traditional family gave support and stability to the union between man and woman. Where everyone lives together, or very near each other – cousins, brothers and sisters, grandparents, uncles and aunts – there are perhaps fewer confrontations between the man and the woman because they are not alone, face to face with each other. Their relationships are diffused by the group. In the nuclear family, on the other hand, the husband and wife, together with their children, often find themselves very isolated. If their relationship is not one of sharing and sensitivity, it can deteriorate very quickly. For a relationship to remain alive, energy, creativity and time are needed. But so many couples live in situations where they no longer have the energy to deepen their relationship, and this causes them to drift apart.

The relationship between them is so precious, not only for the two of them but also for the children, for society, for God, that the Father himself has promised always to come and help them as they journey towards a more profound unity. This union between man and woman is sacred. It is in the image of God, the Father, Son and Spirit. It is, above all, the first human union, the source of all other human unions.

MARRIAGE AS A SACRAMENT

This is why the union of man and woman is a sacrament. It is announced before the Church and confirmed by the Church. It is a sacred sign, instituted by Jesus. It is a place of encounter with God; he is present in this union and always comes to the aid of the spouses. He helps them to profit from all the difficult elements in marriage. Instead of hiding from each other and escaping into work or other activities; instead of becoming aggressive or depressive, they can live a deeper union through the acceptance of daily life with one another. They can live not only the deep joys of this union, but also forgiveness.

Forgiveness is the great gift of Jesus to humanity. Jesus came to pardon us and to show us how to forgive. Forgiveness is the love offered to another who is wounded, vulnerable, fearful and who has broken the unity. Forgiveness implies the understanding that all the blockages, all the aggressive acts come, in great measure, from inner sufferings, anguish, and fears. Forgiveness is the welcome of the other just as he or she is with all the flaws, all the past, all the weaknesses, and all the sin. Forgiveness signifies and acknowledges the covenant with another.

It is this forgiveness coming from the heart of God which heals people in the depths of their being. It is this which progressively transforms the wounded image of self into the positive image of a child of God. It is this which transforms culpability into responsibility and into confidence in oneself, in others, and in God. When one has experienced this forgiveness, he or she is able in turn to forgive.

The sacrament of marriage transforms the foundations of the union between man and woman. It is not only a question of love one for the other, of the promise to give oneself to another for life, but a call and a confirmation of God. The foundations of this union are in the desire of the Father that man and woman, despite their wounds and their psychological and human poverty, should share in his trinitarian life and in his merciful love. The life of the couple, then, is founded on this forgiveness which alone can heal the wounds inflicted on their unity. The road to unity must pass through daily forgiveness. And celebration, which is a sign that forgiveness is total, culminates in the tenderness and union of love. This union of love in spirit and body drives out all aggression and the blockages which might remain, and makes of the two one flesh, one heart, one soul, one spirit ... The union becomes eucharistic, an act of thanksgiving for having refound unity.

This is why the genital organs are sacred. They are reserved for a divine work: to be at the same time a sign of trinitarian life and a source of life. These organs must be used only to live a life of love and a covenant which has been blessed and confirmed by God himself. Their usage outside this covenant traps the man and the woman each in his or her own isolation. The sexual act, instead of being a source and sign of hope, becomes a cause of despair. It awakens that which is most intimate, most sacred, most vulnerable in the human heart without being able to fulfil it, or to respond to the deep need to be loved with a total love. Only when it is enveloped in the presence of Jesus can the love of husband and wife deepen and bring them profound peace. Their hearts are thirsting, not for a passing love, not for a subjective pleasure, but for a total and eternal love which will bring them out of their isolation into unity.

The tragedy of marriage and the union of bodies in love is that so many enter into it believing that it is going to be paradise and that their deepest needs will be fulfilled. Others, who have had bad experiences, may enter into marriage with cynicism and despair. Truth lies between these two attitudes, between naivety and despair. The human heart thirsts for a paradise and an eternal wedding feast which is not illusory, but one can only enter into happiness in stages. So many of the young who lack maturity believe that perhaps marriage will be this paradise. But they discover that it is a school of life and love. Progressively, through the joys and the ecstasies, but also through the sufferings, the blockages, and forgiving each other, they learn how to love and be faithful. At first, the gift of their tenderness and their bodies is very immature. But because they want their union to be a sign of the presence of God and a sacrament, they grow together in love and truth. Together they become a sign of the Kingdom. United Christian families are a sign that love, unity and peace are possible. These families are, each in their own way, the first cell of all unity, of all forgiveness, of all community, of all fecundity. They are thus signs of hope.

MARRIAGE FOR PEOPLE WITH A MENTAL HANDICAP

It is evident that some people with a mental handicap, especially if it is slight, are able to enter into the joys and pains of a conjugal life and of a family life. However, many have been labelled 'deficient' or 'disabled'. In reality, they could have functioned quite well in society if they had received adequate support. But being categorized as 'deficient' deeply wounds a person and destroys self-confidence. This negative image, of being one who is considered 'different', 'abnormal', is confirmed by parents, by others around and, finally, by placement in a special centre.

A study carried out by Jacques Servais on the support needed by those with a mental handicap who marry, seems to me to be the most comprehensive; it provides many examples and a bibliography.[2] It confirms perfectly the experience of the communities of l'Arche, that marriage is possible, but only for a minority of those with a mental handicap.

The right to marry, an inalienable right of everyone, can only be exercised lawfully and lived fully, if its duties express the will to respect the partner of the covenant. Moreover, as with all vocations, marriage presupposes attractions and aptitudes. In contemporary society, the accent is generally put on the attraction for marriage rather than on the aptitude. Here, as elsewhere, educators must try to motivate the partners with mental handicaps to take responsibility for their future. To do

2. 'Jalons pour l'accompagnement au mariage des personnes handicapées', thesis by Jacques Servais, presented at the University of Louvain la Neuve, 1981.

this, they must begin by creating a relationship of trust which engenders security, then they can bring constructive criticism and help to the two concerned.[3]

A guide or a counsellor is needed to help clarify what is hidden in the desire which has been expressed for marriage, to explain fully the real responsibilities it entails and to ensure that the capacity to face them is developed. Because, as we all know, marriage is never easy. It is a place of growth and flowering for the two spouses.

The guide will have the task of stimulating social, friendly and familial relationships in order to keep the couple from closing in on themselves. The roles of such a guide are manifold: to serve as a reference, confidant or counsellor if requested by the couple: perhaps above all to renew confidence in times of difficulty.

In spite of all the problems, statistics and research reveal that there are no more separations or divorces among marriages of those with mental handicaps than among those regarded as 'normal'.[4] But behind the figures there are very different, and sometimes suffering, realities.

I remember the situation of Paul and Marie. Marie is a woman of about forty who is paralysed down one side and had lived in one of our communities for four years. She was difficult, finding it hard to live in a group if she was not continually the centre of attention, and she knew well how to get it.

Before coming to the community, she had lived at home: a traditional family in which, because of her handicap, she had always been hidden. There was no question of her going out to a dance or to visit friends as her younger brothers and sister did. And because of this Marie was angry and bitter. She was never satisfied. Because of her handicap, her capacity for work was limited, but she dreamed of an independent life. She insisted that the team find her an apartment in the city, although there was no certainty that she was ready for such autonomy. Very quickly, Marie met a man who was also handicapped and had lived in one of our homes but was now living in an apartment and holding a job in competitive employment. They quickly moved in together without telling anyone.

3. ibid., p. 27.
4. ibid., p. 113.

We didn't know what to do. Marie had already had several relationships with men when she lived in the community home. In general, these men were much younger and more limited than she was; her love for them was terribly possessive. These relationships were always harmful for the men concerned.

We did not know if Marie was capable of fidelity. Did she love Paul for himself, or was she simply seeking the status of a 'married woman'? In addition, they both had problems with alcohol. It was difficult to know how to guide them when both, in a very understandable adolescent crisis, affirmed their autonomy by rejecting everyone who came to them from the community. It was then that a couple, friends of the community, befriended them and were able to give them support. Paul and Marie decided to marry. The attitude of Marie's family completely changed once she 'became like everyone else'; she found her place, an equality with her brothers and sister. The first years of the marriage were difficult. Marie finding herself alone all day in the apartment, began to drink more and more. She finally agreed to take part in a detoxification programme, and, for the last two years, their marriage has been much more peaceful.

On reading a report about people placed in a hospital for mentally deficient people (Pacific State Hospital, California),[5] and then being discharged, I was surprised at how many had married more or less successfully. Of the forty-eight people studied, all with fairly mild handicaps, thirty-four had married. Only four of this group have separated from their partner or been divorced. The story of each one is different, but there are certain constants. Those who had been very disturbed at a sexual level before their entry into the hospital, had found inner stability and peace in a committed relationship; and each manifested a certain pride in having a home of their own, a husband or wife. Nearly all the women had been sterilized before they were discharged from the hospital, and they suffered from this. There is no doubt that their desire to escape the label of mental deficiency, and to be like everyone else, was the strength which helped them to live in marriage. The anguish of loneliness immediately after they had left the hospital had also been a force which had

5. Robert B. Edgerton, *The Cloak of Competence*, University of California Press, 1967.

prompted them to seek and to find a possible partner. And, once married, they were so determined not to fall again into this anguish that they often made considerable sacrifices and adjustments for the sake of their marriage. Maybe it is easier for someone with a mental handicap to accept such adjustments than for others more capable, more autonomous, more jealous of their independence and their rights – and less willing to be at the service of the other.

THE CHILD

Obviously, the most delicate question is that of procreation. Can a couple, both of whom have mental handicaps, have children? This question is complex. We quickly forget that some women with mental handicaps long, more than anything, to be mothers. The suffering of sterility is intolerable for them. If they are encouraged to have sexual relationships and are prevented from conceiving a child, their deepest desire is not being met.

However, it must be acknowledged that it is not good for some people with a mental handicap to have a child. Clearly we must not encourage the conception and birth of a child if there is a risk of it being severely handicapped, or not welcomed, loved and cared for. But the problem is not simply a question of heredity. More delicate is the fact that the person with a mental handicap will often not be able to bring up her child even if it is normal. A mother who has a mental handicap is able, of course, to nurse her child and to enjoy looking at him, carrying him, playing with him; but, when the child becomes irritable, difficult, anguished, there is a risk that the mother may become terribly insecure and anguished herself. At that moment, she may abandon or abuse her child. For a mother to bring up her child she must have a security, a liberty, and an interior peace which is often lacking in someone with a mental handicap. It is irresponsible to let someone with a handicap have children whom they are manifestly not able to bring up adequately.

But, there again, we can be mistaken. Emmanuelle became pregnant by Christopher, a man with hemiplegia who had lived in one of our homes and who lacked all confidence in himself. Both he and Emmanuelle worked in the same workshop. The staff there urged Emmanuelle to have an abortion. She refused.

She absolutely wanted her baby. Christopher was very frightened; he was so lacking in confidence that he didn't believe he could be a husband, let alone a father. But, little by little, he became more peaceful and the two of them decided to marry. Christopher accepted the idea of being a father. Some time before all this, Christopher had left his home in l'Arche, refusing all contact with the assistants. He wanted to go it alone. But, faced with Emmanuelle's pregnancy, the questions of his marriage, and the idea of being a father, he sought out the assistants for counsel and support. Christopher and Emmanuelle are now happy parents. A couple, friends of the community, visit them on a regular basis. A deep friendship has been established between the two couples. They help each other. Their little child seems happy. He is growing up well, and Christopher and Emmanuelle seem to be excellent parents. It is beautiful to see them.

Jacqueline was in one of our city homes. She became pregnant by a man whom we had welcomed on a trial basis in another home and whom we did not know well. We found a foster home for Jacqueline. Through becoming a mother she made much progress; she became more independent and found work in a factory near her home, something she had not been capable of doing before the birth of her child. She lived with her child; but the couple who had welcomed her acted as parents. This situation, though by no means perfect, was not too bad. It was a human situation. The little one grew and soon surpassed his mother on the intellectual level. This threatened her, and she began to regret having him. Was this the reason she became pregnant a second time, probably by someone at the factory? In speaking with her during this second pregnancy, it seemed evident that she did not wish to bring up her second child. He was born, a beautiful baby, and adopted very young. Then the woman who had welcomed Jacqueline died, and the elderly husband was no longer able to keep her and her first child whom she could no longer tolerate. We found a centre, not far away, which welcomed her first child who is helped by his godfather, a former assistant of l'Arche who was with us during Jacqueline's first pregnancy. We also had to find another foster family for Jacqueline. The situation remains delicate. Is not this the fragility inherent in the human condition? Jacqueline is surrounded with competent care; it is necessary to continue to walk closely with her.

Michelle sought her independence from the community. She is an intelligent young woman but very wounded in her heart and emotions, and abandoned by her family. When we welcomed her twelve years ago, she was close to psychosis. She has made much progress at a human and social level and in her work. For some time, she has lived alone, working in a factory. She was very happy to be finally on her own, free, 'not having assistants on her back'! But she was seduced by an older man who took advantage of her. She had been attracted to this man who needed her. They did not live together, but they saw each other regularly. She conceived a child and had an abortion. Speaking of this one day with a former assistant, she told her story with a little defiance and pride, insinuating that she was much freer than the assistant. When the assistant asked her whether she had not suffered, Michelle burst into tears, admitting that she had been forced to have the abortion.

I know of three other situations, in l'Arche communities, where women have had children. We are always against abortion. First, because it is serious to kill a child in its mother's womb; and, secondly, because the women themselves have not wanted abortions. It is often the educators and parents who do not want a woman for whom they are responsible to have a child and who manipulate her so that she accepts the abortion. In these three cases (which is very few considering the number of people we have welcomed into our communities and the fact that we do not give contraceptives), the women have given birth to beautiful children. They were able to touch them, to look at them, to admire them, and even to give them a name. In all three situations, the mothers agreed that their little one be adopted.

It is wrong to encourage a young pregnant woman to have an abortion. This causes her to believe that the fruit of her womb is rotten. If her fruit is rotten, then she herself must be rotten. This reinforces the broken image she has of herself and forces her to live with serious guilt. To force her to abort is to cut off the movement of life within her.

It is obvious that all of this is not simple. We are touching an area where there is much human suffering and fragility. I still have many questions on this difficult subject regarding the possibility of those with a mental handicap having children. Each situation depends so much on the history and the character of each person that it seems to me well nigh impossible to lay down rigid rules.

How can we help a couple who cannot have children or, if they could, are not able to raise a child adequately, to avoid closing in on themselves as so often happens. Will they find, instead of welcome and service of the child which is the natural fruit of a couple, the necessary resources to make their life in common a life open to others and to God? What is the source of strength and hope which will allow them to come to terms with their differences, overcome the conflicts and surpass the difficulties and blockages which are found in daily life? I think that a common ideal, which places their life as a couple in a perspective of service, close to a community which will support and motivate them, will give them the best chance to achieve and maintain balance and maturity.

In this area there are many unanswered questions. I think in particular of Didier and Marianne who both have emotional difficulties and intellectual deficiencies. I wouldn't dare to say that they were capable of raising a child. Yet their marriage has brought them both a real well-being and a new stability. They love each other and support each other. Even if there are difficulties, these do not prevent their marriage from being positive.

WHO CAN GET MARRIED?

Finally then, who can be encouraged towards marriage? First, one point must be clear: it must be the couple themselves who decide to marry, never the decision of someone else. In l'Arche we do not speak of marriage to those who, in the abstract, wish to marry. We speak of it to a couple who have already made their own way towards it. Certainly, someone is able to envisage marriage only if he or she is moving toward a real emotional maturity, passing from the stage of attracting everyone to oneself to the stage of opening oneself to another or others, toward a real responsibility for them. This emotional maturity implies that, gradually, the person is becoming capable of a permanent relationship with another person, capable also of helping the other and carrying someone who is in some way weaker.

Of course, there is no such thing as a perfectly self-giving and altruistic love; we always seek in another something for ourselves. Closed in on ourselves, we have a hard time listening and understanding others, and we are even in danger of oppressing and destroying them. But there can be a gradual liberation from egotistical tendencies. Little by little we can be opened as we discover the other as a living person, who has needs and who suffers, a person whom we can help to grow in inner equilibrium and to discover the truth of his or her being, a person we can love and be loved by.

Personally, I have great confidence in those couples who, announcing their desire to marry, take the time to deepen the meaning of their marriage without hastily moving into sexual relations, and who are willing to have someone accompany and counsel them.

Thus, the time of their engagement becomes a time of deepening discovery of the other, through the heart and through dialogue in which they are able to share their ideas of life, their tastes, their desires, their values. They have time to look at some questions before they arise, perhaps in crisis or urgency, in their life as a couple. They are able to reflect together on the changes which will take place in their lives and on the best way to experience these together; this takes place through a course of preparation adapted to their needs and guided by a supportive friend. During this time they can also receive a more complete sexual education which would permit them to know and respect the other more, and to discover the mysterious and sacred dimension of genital sexuality.

If the couple places their union under God through the sacrament of marriage, not in order to have 'a beautiful celebration', but because of their trust in God and the Church, then I am even more confident. God works such marvels in poor and simple hearts!

And a human being, often so poor and fragile, is so rich in unexpected possibilities for growth.

8

Fecundity and the Welcome of Death

THE CRY FOR FECUNDITY

No one can deny that the body of man, like that of woman, was made as it is in order to maintain humanity on the earth. Their differences and their mutual attraction are necessary for life to give life. There is an obvious link between genital sexuality and procreation. This link is so profound, that for a long time the moralists and theologians acknowledged only fecundity as the real end of sexual union, leaving the expression of intimate love in the shadows. On the other hand, in our times, the connection between sexual relationships and intimacy has been so accentuated that people forget the link between genital sexuality and the fear of death. They refuse to acknowledge the physical and deeply rooted need to leave behind us another like ourselves, a living being which has come forth from our own living body. In our rich society, there is a real link between the refusal or fear of death and the refusal and fear of fecundity, of fruitfulness. The desire for procreation, the yearning for a child, is contained in genital sexuality. Genital sexuality certainly responds to the intention of Yahweh to save us from our fear of isolation: 'It is not good that man should be alone.' It also responds to another intention of Yahweh in warding off our fear of another isolation, that of death: 'Be fruitful and multiply' (Genesis 1:28).

Even when one refuses to have a child, the cry and the desire of nature is so strong and powerful, that despite all precautions, despite all natural or artificial means of contraception, there are still an immense number of children who are conceived and, alas, aborted.

Biological life is made up of three functions: assimilation, growth, and procreation. Assimilation permits growth by the multiplication of the cells. All growth is directed towards

137

procreation in order that the species continues to exist. All living beings have the means of reproduction and an insatiable need to give life. This need is so powerful that, from generation to generation, vegetation, animals, and human beings reproduce and perpetuate life on earth. Those of ancient cultures saw in this something divine. The living, said Plato and Aristotle, are not immortal in themselves; the individual is mortal, but he participates in immortality through the species, by his capacity to reproduce another like himself. The desire for immortality is hidden in the cry or the desire for reproduction, for procreation.

The mystery of fecundity implies the desire of the seed to rest in the bosom of the earth and the desire of the earth to welcome the seed and to nourish it. This physical, psychological and metaphysical desire for reproduction, for procreation, for childbirth is a sign of God hidden in living matter. It is the secret of God confided to living beings, written into their biological reality. In the attraction of man for woman, and of woman for man, in their loving attention, there is something divine, a thirst for immortality, a desire for fecundity.

There is something extraordinarily beautiful in the conception of a child, but also something so very little and humble. From the moment of fertilization, the mother in some sense has nothing more to do except to let the process of life continue within her. She cannot even choose the sex of her child.

In human fecundity, biological fecundity is fulfilled by the fecundity of love and caring. It is necessary that the parents welcome with love and tenderness the little one whom they have conceived so that the child can grow and find his or her place in the universe. Human fecundity does not end at birth as is also the case with more evolved animals. Parents continue through long years to carry their child, giving life and nourishment and helping him or her to grow in so many ways. It is the parents' love and care which gives the baby security to overcome fear and anguish; it is their love which allows the child, in spite of so much fragility and vulnerability, to find its place in the family, and thus in society and in the world.

When we see to what extent children become mentally and psychically blocked, either because of rejection or because of over-protection, we can easily understand how real love must be a source of life. One who is loved is able to grow without fear, able to be him or herself and acquire language to communicate, and above all, to develop the capacity to love others.

Sterility is a terrible tragedy for a human being. In psychiatric hospitals and in institutions for chronically sick people, we find women who have deliberately made themselves ugly; they dress badly, their hair is a mess, they smell awful: they are so sure that no one could love them, and that they are sterile and incapable of giving life! In ancient civilizations, sterility was sometimes considered a punishment from God. But if biological sterility is painful, spiritual sterility is even more terrible.

Productivity should not be confused with fecundity. Productivity resembles fecundity, but they are very different. We produce, using reason and techniques, an object which does not live. It is a material object to be possessed, used or sold, but it is never an end in itself. Productivity gives power to those who control production.

To be fruitful, to bear fruit, is to give life to another human being. It is a relationship, in love, of one living being with another. We do not possess the one to whom we give life. On the contrary, we give the child space to live; we give him or her freedom. It is marvellous to be fruitful; but, there is a risk involved. We cannot do as we like with our child. The situation becomes tragic when parents want to programme and control the whole life of their child. This can provoke mental sickness. Fecundity implies entering into the whole chain of life which links human beings together throughout history. The child must inevitably overtake its parents in some way and in turn be overtaken by his or her own children. Life is a continual discovery, uncovering in wonder and unending newness the secrets of God. The history of humanity is holy because in it the mystery of God is revealed through love and through the struggle against the forces of evil, darkness and falsehood. An education which is too programmed, is based on fear; fecundity, in contrast, is based on trust in life and in the Source of all life.

It is essential for all human beings to discover and to live their fecundity. Through this they will penetrate to the heart of God, to the heart of divine fecundity which is the Holy Spirit.

All human beings long to continue beyond death. They need to know that at their death they will not simply leave an empty bed in a hospital or an asylum, but that they will continue to live somewhere, that their memory, their life, their spirit will be

perpetuated. Thus they will live in those to whom they have given life, in those whose hearts they have awakened and opened to a greater love, and in those to whom they have communicated the mystery of God.

For a human being, the awareness of his or her fecundity allows him or her in part to overcome the fear of death. Fecundity consists in the gift which contributes to the fullness of the physical, spiritual and divine life of another, to his or her joy in living and existing, and growing to complete fulfilment. The awareness of one's fecundity is to know that one day someone will look at me and say: 'If I am alive and happy, it is because of you!' It is the joy of knowing that I, too, am able to cry out to so many others: 'Thank you! If I live and if I am happy, it is thanks to you!' Fecundity is to know that we are all interdependent and that we are able to communicate to others our love, our trust, our hope, our faith, our joy and our peace. Someone closed up and moody will make all those around him closed up and moody. Fear gives birth to fear, aggression to aggression. Tenderness engenders tenderness; confidence engenders confidence, and kindness, kindness. I love that phrase that Abbé Pierre, founder of the international Emmaus communities, says so often: 'It is necessary to be contagious with hope.'

Yet, some people seem to be so deeply blocked inside. Life does not flow harmoniously within them. It is as if they were cut off from the world of their own feelings. Often they are very productive or gifted intellectually, but they do not give life. They are not able to listen to others, to sense their sufferings and needs, to relax with them. To be fruitful it is necessary to find a certain wholeness and inner harmony, and to be in touch with the source of one's being and the world of one's deepest feelings. Usually, this requires that a person must enter again the anguish which was unbearable during childhood, and for some this means reliving very deep sufferings. This is only possible if they are accompanied by someone who is both compassionate and competent, and who remains very committed to them.

FRUITFULNESS AND CELIBACY

Loving parents are able to discover and live their fecundity. They have the joy of being called 'Daddy' and 'Mummy'. It is more difficult for celibates – those who are unmarried by choice and those unable to marry – to discover their fruitfulness. There are so many men and women who have known rejection, and have felt they were a disappointment and a burden to their parents, and to whom no one has revealed their capacity to give life and be fruitful. Instead, they have been made to feel that they were bothering others and even that they brought anguish and death instead of life. They have been separated from the family milieu. Those who have been so deeply rejected sense that life has no meaning, since they have nothing to bring to others.

When people are unable to marry, and know the feeling 'no one wants me', they suffer terribly from an experience of sterility. This sterility proves to them that they are no good. This is the case with Georgette, of whom I spoke in chapter 1, who said 'I will never be able to marry because my mother said that if I married, I might have a child like me.' This is the hidden message in a forced abortion: 'Your fruit is rotten. The tree which is you is also rotten.' It is wrong to put the young in situations where one forbids them to be fruitful, implying in the same breath that they are bad. Today, there are those who, in the name of liberty, proclaim the right to sexual pleasure for people with a handicap. But, at the same time, if they should conceive a child, it is considered virtually a crime.

If we judge someone as incapable of having a child, then we must be truthful. We must help the person to discover how he or she is able to be truly fruitful, to give life, but in another way. Each one of us has the right to find our own true fecundity.

The fundamental question, at l'Arche, for those who are not able to establish a family, is how to find meaning in their lives and true fecundity. Without this their bodies will always cry out in physiological need and their hearts will continue to live with that sense of sterility. They will seek to appease the anguish of isolation through pleasure and distractions. If, however, their human and spiritual fecundity has been revealed to them, their bodies will no longer hunger in the same way. The role of l'Arche, and of all those who are close to people with a handicap, is to help them to discover that their life has a meaning, that the community, the Church, society has need of them; that they have a very special capacity to touch hearts and to give life.

Many of us at l'Arche, and many of those who are near to

those with a handicap, have lived through this experience. We have discovered how our own hearts have been awakened by the person with a handicap. We have experienced a profound healing coming from the confidence, the spontaneity, the love and simple affection of a person who is intellectually poor.

A short time ago, a Jesuit director sent a very competent, but anguished man to a l'Arche community in Canada. Speaking of him, he told me: 'The unconditional welcome by the people of the community so staggered him that, after a year, he returned a changed man. He still has his anguishes, but he has learnt to accept them better.' This is one example among thousands of people who have been healed and transformed by those with a mental handicap.

However, to be fruitful requires two people. No one can be fruitful alone. It is the reality of the seed and the earth, of the man and the woman. Biological fecundity demands that there be two. It is the same with spiritual fecundity. A child grows harmoniously when he feels loved by two people, drawn into the circle of love which flows between the father and the mother.[1] In the Christian vision of sexuality, man and woman render present the mystery of the Trinity. Our God is not a solitary God; he is one God in three Persons. In fecundity, there is also a trinitarian mystery.

THE FRUITFULNESS OF THE COMMUNITY

If it is true that, in order to be fruitful, it is necessary to be two; we must ask ourselves what is the fecundity of the community in which people with a handicap live. First of all, such people have an amazing capacity to create community life, a capacity that people more developed intellectually do not usually have. At l'Arche, we have often been astonished to hear the reflections of visitors: 'It does me so much good to be with you. Living continually in the big city, I am constantly under pressure; I have to create barriers to protect myself. Here, for the first time, I feel liberated because I am so welcomed.'

Those with a mental handicap have fewer barriers around

1. In chapter 2 we have spoken of how difficult it is for the single parent to bring up a child.

their hearts. They do not live in the world of ideas and theories. They are down-to-earth and do not try to defend their position, their place in the social scale. Often they live outside the conventions of politeness. They do not look at visitors in terms of their qualifications or what they do. They are drawn to the heart, to the person who exists behind the mask. It is because they live close to the values of the heart that they find their place in the community. They know how to love, to celebrate, to live joyfully there, while intellectuals and those who are normally self-assured are often ill at ease.

Recently a Canadian, who had been an assistant in l'Arche fourteen years earlier, came back to see us. I had completely forgotten him. It was Alfred who threw himself into his arms: he remembered his name, and where he had worked. The former assistant was very touched. Those with a mental handicap have an amazing capacity for welcome. They give life and warmth; they know how to recognize another person and his or her needs.

At l'Arche, we often make pilgrimages and journeys in small groups. Everywhere we are welcomed, and we are surprised by the remarks: 'There is something in your group which is so simple and glowing that we are warmed and comforted by it.'

At Easter 1981, there was a 'Faith and Light' pilgrimage to Lourdes. We were about 12,000 pilgrims: 4,000 young people and friends, 4,000 people with handicaps and 4,000 parents, representing 350 communities of 'Faith and Light' across the world. It was an explosion of joy. On Easter Sunday in the afternoon, there was a great celebration on the Basilica Esplanade. From all corners of the city, the communities paraded to the meeting. Everyone wore a poncho – of different colours and different styles. It was the great celebration of the poor and the weak. They came, some in wheelchairs, some walking with difficulty, some very disfigured; but all, or nearly all, smiling, cheering and shouting with joy.

The next morning a television camerman asked me: 'How do you explain all this? I like my job, I have money, but they have something I don't have. They have joy.' I responded by quoting from the Gospel: 'The stone which the builders rejected has become the cornerstone.' If handicapped and rejected people are really accepted as they are, they become the heart of the community, and of society. They renew the community by their simplicity and their trust: they ease tensions and bring down barriers. Human beings, instead of being rivals, are then able to co-operate so that those who are the most poor can grow and truly take their place in the world.

When people with a handicap find meaning to their lives, through and in a truly loving community, they become fruitful. They are no longer 'handicapped'; they are just people amongst others in the community, having their own unique gift which others do not have. Then there is no longer any need for jealousy. Each one has found his or her place. The difference between people is no longer a threat, a source of envy, jealousy or rivalry, but has become rather a source of richness. Together we constitute a 'body', open and welcoming where we can be ourselves.

Of course, it is necessary at the same time to help those with a handicap to progress, to develop to the maximum their potential for autonomy, for work, for service. It would be very wrong if, under the pretext that each one has a unique gift and that those with a handicap have, above all, a gift of the heart, we impeded the development of their latent abilities.

For those with a mental handicap to discover their fruitfulness in the community, they must find others who want to live with them and are willing to let themselves be touched in the depths of their hearts by them. The presence of friendly visitors is also important, if they have learnt to lower barriers built around their hearts. Those with mental handicaps are so often set aside; it is so easy to refuse to look at them or listen to them; it is so easy to be scornful.

In some institutions which I have visited, there is often a great gulf between the staff and the handicapped people. The latter are not really helped to discover their true fecundity, because of the lack of hope in those around them. The staff do not seem to believe in the fecundity of those with a handicap. Sometimes they even hinder it. They find it convenient to plant them in front of the television, which makes them passive. They do not encourage those who are handicapped to exercise their gifts, their capacities of welcome and for relationship, because there is no one to welcome. Sometimes they encourage sexual relations amongst them, but they refuse them biological fecundity and have no concern for their human and spiritual fecundity.

SPIRITUAL FECUNDITY

The spiritual fecundity of someone with a mental handicap who lives in a community of faith deepens even more when he or she has had a certain experience of God. I am astonished by the capacity for faith in those with a mental handicap, whether they are Moslems, Hindus, Protestants or Roman Catholics. There is something in their openness to God which touches me deeply. Having less capacity for reason, they have a greater capacity for trust. Some live with the trust which we find in a child and which is sometimes destroyed in a more sophisticated person, who may become cynical. Those with a mental handicap often find it hard to verbalize what goes on within them, but many seem to enjoy a tranquility and a true interior peace at the moment of prayer, during the liturgy, or after communion. Some who have severe handicaps, experience long moments of serenity during liturgical celebrations although at other times they are constantly agitated. This is a sign that they are living something true and very profound inside themselves. Perhaps they are discovering their interior beauty, finding their true place in the heart of the Church and the universe, in the Heart of God. Through this real experience of God – which is given to them and remains hidden from the intellectuals, the over-active and those too concerned about their status and place in society, they seem to discover their true identity.

A few years ago, Yolanda entered into a phase of profound regression. She is an intelligent young woman, but deeply broken. She had been rejected by her family, considered as 'abnormal', put into an institution, sterilized. She had made several attempts at suicide and had a very wounded image of herself and her femininity. She regressed to the point of being like a very small child. She remained as a baby, needing the most elementary care for several weeks. Someone had to be constantly with her. One day, Father Thomas came to give her communion; he prayed with her and whispered something into her ear. For the first time, Yolanda opened her eyes, and smiled. It seemed that this was a moment of breakthrough, the beginning of her return to life. Father Thomas had simply told her that he needed her and her prayer, the offering of her suffering. She sensed this to be true, that he did need her, that she was able to help him bring life to others.

145

When human beings discover that they are truly loved by God
and that they can live a relationship with him, a change takes
place within them. They are no longer disheartened by their
limits and handicaps. By this union with Jesus, they can
communicate life. They are able to believe the words of Jesus:
'Everything you ask of the Father in my name, I will give it to
you.'

I am struck by the way in which the men in my own home
pray for Lebanon and for other areas of distress in the world.
They truly believe that through Jesus they are able to affect a
situation through prayer.

So many handicapped men and women in our homes have
very compassionate hearts. They have an intuition of the sufferings of others. I think of Joan, who herself has suffered much.
She is hemiplegic, and has a poor and awkward body. She would
so love to be married and to have children. One day, I was very
tired. She came close to me and put her hand on my head with
so much tenderness. Then she said to me: 'I love you, you know.'
At that moment, I felt as if I were a little child. She knew how
to warm my heart and to give me life. So many in l'Arche are
deeply happy when they can do something for an elderly person
or someone even more handicapped than they are themselves.
They love to take babies into their arms! Of course, they are
awkward and sometimes they make the babies cry. But their
hearts are so delicate. They want to help so much . . . It is an
essential task, for a community such as ours, to enable each one
to have a responsibility for someone who is weaker.

DIFFICULTIES

It is not simple to find one's true fecundity. Many who have a
mental handicap remain frustrated and dissatisfied. They want
to be like their brothers and sisters who are married. Some want
to go on living with their parents and others desire to live
independently. They have a hard time accepting their handicap,
and their hearts are often filled with anger and frustration. Some
have closed themselves up in a role which is not their real
self. Others are torn between the demands of society, with its
ambivalent values, and their own human, psychic, and spiritual
reality, with all its limits and wounds. The fecundity of these

people is ignored by the world and by themselves. They do not know how to give life through their hearts and their love. Naturally they feel frustrated.

It is not surprising then that so many people with mild mental handicaps or emotional disturbances are torn between the attraction of 'productivity' – with the esteem, the riches, the feelings of superiority that this can bring – and their true fecundity. They do not dare to believe that, in spite of their limits, they can be fruitful and give life. The mass media confirms their doubts and draws them into the productive, competitive and aggressive world. It is not surprising that they are confused.

The task of community is to enter into dialogue with them, carrying their confusion, accepting their aggression and their frustrations. It is a question of hoping against hope with them, for the day when they will be able to go beyond the illusory desire for 'normality' – to be a qualified worker, to have a family, and so on, which is unattainable for them – to the peace which comes from the profound acceptance of oneself and of others. Community life gives each one the possibility of living an encounter with others and with God. Only when one has accepted one's handicap in a realistic way will it be possible to begin to overcome it. This may enable some to take greater responsibility in the community or even to entertain a realistic hope of finding one day someone they can marry.

THE FRUITFULNESS OF SUFFERING

But community must also teach us how to live with those who do not attain this peace and acceptance of themselves. It is my faith in Jesus, in his sufferings and his resurrection, which helps me, with others, to stay close to those who constantly live in suffering and anguish, whose hearts are wounded and broken, whose bodies are disfigured. These are people who have been torn apart by rejection, there is a void in them, filled sometimes by upsurges of aggression or strong sexual impulses. But, in their essence, they too are children of God. The community is called to carry them in faith and to offer, with them, their cries and their sufferings. I believe that there is a mysterious fecundity in suffering. It is difficult to speak of this, because it is a reality which I sense through my faith, and which I can explain only by an analogy: that which is rejected by human beings becomes fertilizing manure; the excrement of animals and of humans is good for the earth. That which is rotten nourishes the earth and helps it to bear fruit, to give life.

I believe that the sufferings of human beings and their poverty are like a cry which ascends to God. In some way, God is present there.

Isaiah says of the suffering servant:

> Without beauty, without majesty,
> no looks to attract our eyes;
> a thing despised and rejected by men,
> a man of sorrows and familiar with suffering,
> a man to make people screen their faces;
> he was despised and we took no account of him.
>
> (Isaiah 53:2–3)

These words can be applied to so many men and women in the world who suffer from rejection, sometimes from their birth, sometimes even from their conception. How can we understand and give meaning to this suffering? Is there a link between the suffering we see in some people in our communities and the following words of Isaiah?

> And yet ours were the sufferings he bore,
> ours the sorrows he carried . . .
> Yet he was pierced through for our faults, . . .
>
> (Isaiah 53:4–5)

Suffering people are often totally unaware that their distress can bear fruit. Perhaps the community, in living with them and their cries, can offer this suffering on their behalf to the Father in the belief that their cries are heard; that the Father makes them fruitful in union with the Passion of his Son.[2]

If we remain at the level of material things, searching only for productivity and possessions, death will appear as the most terrible event for a human being, the most radical break. But, if we place ourselves at the level of fecundity, we will discover that death is a beginning. We can let go of life, for there are bonds with those we leave behind which will remain forever.

2. c.f. *Salvifici Doloris: The Apostolic Letter of John Paul II on Suffering: 11th February 1984.* Catholic Truth Society 1984.

Death will then seem a little less terrifying; it is the return to the Father. In the Christian vision, death is the summit of gift and sacrifice: we give our lives for our friends, and in this we are fruitful.

THE CELEBRATION OF DEATH

A community which knows how to celebrate life and fecundity must also know how to celebrate death. Freud, in *Our Attitude Towards Death*, takes the old Latin adage, 'If you want to preserve peace, arm for war', and transposes it to, 'If you want to endure life, prepare yourself for death'. That is true: if we live in fear of death, if we hide it from ourselves and others, we become anguished by the signs which announce it: sickness, handicaps, diminishing strength, setbacks, a sense that life is passing by. Death is part of the natural cycle. Certainly death, and particularly a brutal death, is a terrible reality; but, at the same time, it is a deeply natural reality, a reality written in our flesh, which so many others before us have lived through and beyond.

There is an intimate link between an anguished sexuality and the fear of death.

If a community knows how to celebrate death with realism and with tenderness, it will be able to assuage the fears of its members with regard to this very fundamental reality. It is not a question of hiding from the ever-present reality of death, nor of 'prettifying' it; that would only be another way of running away from it. It is a question of looking at it with serenity, of speaking about it, of praying and seeking to see it and to live it with the eyes of God. This does not mean a denial of its sorrowful aspect. Grief is a profoundly human, psychological and spiritual reality.

The death of someone we love is always shattering. To love is to carry another within oneself, to keep a special place in one's heart for him or her. This spiritual space is nourished by a physical presence; death, then, tears out a part of our own heart. Those who deny the suffering of death have never truly loved; they live in a spiritual illusion. To celebrate death, then, is not to deny this laceration and the grief it involves; it is to give space to live it, to speak about it, and even to sing of it. It is to give mutual support, looking the reality in the face and placing all in the Heart of God in deep trust. Jesus did not come to abolish suffering and death, but he showed us the way to live them both fruitfully. We must penetrate the mystery of suffering by surrender and sacrifice.

In l'Arche communities, we are often called to face the reality of death. We see both wrenching, cruel, accidental deaths, and sometimes gentler, predictable deaths, anticipated by sickness and failing strength.

There is a way of announcing a death to the community which brings peace. In our community we speak together of the one who has left us in a vigil of prayer. Wherever possible we keep watch with the body and give an important place to the funeral Mass. In November, the month when, traditionally, we commemorate those who have died, we talk together and share our memories of them. We take time to visit the graves of parents and to pray there. Trying to hide the reality of death is risky and can create very deep-seated fears. It is important to be free to speak of our fears, and in speaking we begin the process of liberation from them.

I remember Francis and Peter, two men with mental and physical handicaps. Both had difficulty in walking. They went to keep watch with Frederick's body, an assistant who had died from cancer after a long illness and whom we had been able to keep in l'Arche during the last months of his life after the doctors could no longer do anything for him in the hospital. Francis was especially touched and he cried out: 'Oh, he is beautiful! He is smiling. Can I kiss him?' He kissed Frederick on his forehead and then exclaimed: 'Oh, he is cold!' And he chuckled quietly. He left, saying to Peter: 'Mummy is going to be surprised when I tell her I kissed a dead person.'

When we realize that the refusal to accept our own handicap is, in part, a refusal of our own death, we can recognize how far Francis and Peter had progressed on that day in the welcome of their own profound and heavy handicaps, for they had approached death in a realistic, simple and peaceful way.

FECUNDITY AND STERILIZATION

Is there a link between sterilization and death? I am deeply disturbed by the number of parents today who seek sterilization for their child. It is frequently a matter of course in the United States and Canada. It is a serious injustice to so mutilate someone, especially when it is done without even asking the person's permission.

Some time ago, in Canada, a mother came to see me. Her daughter was in an apartment where men and women lived together, and the mother came for my advice because she was afraid that there might be 'an accident'. She asked me: 'Shouldn't I have her sterilized?' She helped me to understand the suffering and confusion of so many parents. Not only do they live with the disappointment and suffering of having a child with a mental handicap, but they are rarely helped or supported in dealing with the implications. So many parents today, without being over-protective, are justifiably concerned about the sexual permissiveness propagated throughout the rich countries, where individualism is so accentuated.

I know of staff members in some institutions who, on the grounds of furthering the well-being and liberation of handicapped people, believe without question that it is right to encourage indiscriminate sexual relations, regularly handing out contraceptives and advocating abortion in the case of an 'accident'. Physical union comes to be considered as the normal expression of a relationship. There are even theories advanced which advocate the utilization of genital sexuality as a 'therapy'.

I am sure that these permissive attitudes will have serious consequences because, instead of considering and developing the capacities for love and relationship in those with a handicap, they risk imprisoning them in the search for pleasure for themselves, which finally isolates them more than ever.

When a Christian mother learns that in her daughter's residence there is such sexual permissiveness, how can she protest, knowing that, as a parent, she often has in fact no real possibility of choosing an alternative?

Other reasons for justifying irreversible sterilization are put forward. One day, a mother told me that she had had her daughter sterilized because there was danger in the area where they lived that her daughter might be abused. I had the impression that, for the mother, the most terrible thing that could happen would be for her daughter to conceive a child. She did not seem concerned about, or even aware of, the terrible trauma her daughter might suffer if she were violated. If there was a real danger of rape, should she not think rather of moving to another area or, at least, of seeing that her daughter was always accompanied? She should not leave her alone in the face of such a danger.

It is true, of course, that there are some mothers who are overly concerned about sexuality, for their daughters in particular, and who are unable to trust even the best team of educators.

What a responsibility for the Christian community! There are so few places today which welcome people for long periods, in the spirit of the Gospels, and which wish to help the person with a handicap to develop their real fruitfulness. Why don't Christians react by creating more communities, where the poorest and the weakest are welcomed and respected in their deepest convictions?

The Church is right to remind us of the great principles of life and of fecundity. But it must also cry out for men and women of our world to welcome truly those who, because of their fragility, have no place. It is only if such persons are truly loved through their crises, their aggression and their sufferings, that their broken affectivity will be gradually healed and that they will move toward a greater maturity and a more developed sense of the needs of others.

It is important for our world that there should be much more solidarity between families.

Some time ago, during a retreat, a couple came to see me; the wife was pregnant. Twelve doctors had each diagnosed a high probability that the brain of the child would be profoundly damaged. All twelve had advised them to have an abortion. Some even told them that it was their duty to have an abortion rather than bring into the world a being who would suffer all its life and would cause suffering to future brothers and sisters. They asked my opinion. I told them that I could not accept the idea of killing a child, even a sick one. I promised them, rather vaguely, that I would help them if the child was born with a handicap. Later they met the priest who was responsible for the retreat house where we had been. He told the couple: 'If the baby is handicapped and if you are unable to keep it, I will take

the child into my community and we will take care of it.' With
that assurance, the mother decided not to have an abortion.
Some months later, she gave birth to twins, both perfectly
healthy.

In our world, families must learn more and more how to
welcome someone who is suffering and in distress. But so many
people, so many families, are locked up in prisons of individualism and egoism ... They refuse to welcome, to open their
homes. They are shut up in themselves. Sometimes they do not
even want their own children. They see them as a disturbance
to their material happiness. These families kill their own
fecundity; they are enclosed in sadness and they hinder the
fruitfulness of others. Is a renewal possible?

I believe that there is a profound bond between the love of the
couple and fecundity. True love is necessarily fruitful. So often
the Church is criticized for its position on contraceptives, sterilization and abortion. But above all, the Church exalts human
love; it believes profoundly in the beauty of sexual relationships.
There is something deeply sacred and mysterious in the love of
a husband and a wife, so sacred that this love is celebrated in a
book of Scripture inspired by the Holy Spirit, the Song of Songs.
That love is the sign and the image of the love of God.

But that love was not given to enclose man and woman in an
illusory ghetto. It was given to open one to the other, to God,
to others; it opens the couple most of all to the child, the fruit
of their love.

The relationship between man and woman is obviously
different from those between male and female animals. Between
man and woman there is friendship which precedes and which
follows the sexual relation, and the child has need during long
years for the loving presence of its two parents. The love between
spouses can be expressed without any intention or natural possibility of conceiving a child. The woman, in fact, is fertile for
only a few days each month and only up to a certain age. The
hearts and bodies of the man and the woman are made in such a
way that they are able to show love without biological fecundity.
However, their union must always further a spiritual and human
fecundity and bring to birth a greater love in the hearts of one
for the other, for the children, and for those for whom they are
responsible. The knowledge of the rhythms of fertility oblige the

man and the woman to bear these times of holding back, of waiting. The union of their bodies is so sacred that it demands a readiness to wait and a degree of preparation which is sometimes difficult.

The Church perceives the sacred aspect of this union of bodies in tenderness and it senses the gravity of artificial manipulation of fertility. It fears that this manipulation will lead to the desecration of this love and thus to its death. It also fears that artificial interference will alter the natural functions of the organs of fecundity, which play their role in opening people to one another. Man and woman are like God, through their love for each other, through their fidelity to one another and through their fruitfulness.

9

Celebration of Unity

THE MEANING OF PLEASURE

Today people talk a lot about the right to pleasure for those with a mental handicap; there is less said of their right to be loved and respected in the totality of their being, and their right to have a fruitful and meaningful life.

Aristotle defined pleasure as that which accompanies an activity exercised without interference. There is the pleasure of discussion, the pleasure of work, the pleasure of eating, the pleasure of singing. Each activity engenders its own pleasure. When we do something well, we have a certain awareness of our being, of being alive. The more an activity is good and well done, the more intense the pleasure which accompanies it. In order for human beings to be fully happy, they must be able to develop their capacities to the maximum and they must be able to exercise their activities without hindrance.

It is difficult to learn how to play the piano. But someone who knows how to play does so with pleasure. Psychologists define pleasure as the result of desires that are fulfilled or satisfied. This implies that a person who is unable to exercise even the least activity in an appropriate way is in a state of sadness, of emptiness, and of anguish.

Without pleasure, or at least, without activity, we die. The energies of life no longer flow, but turn around in endless circles. This is anguish. Energy, when it is no longer constructive and creative, becomes destructive.

If people come to l'Arche not knowing how to work or not wanting to work, and if they are disturbed and have difficulties at home, then they will seek satisfaction where they can, maybe through food or masturbation. Some people take pleasure from the negative; it is in opposing and provoking others that they

155

feel they exist. Children who do not receive loving attention will seek an aggressive attention; they would rather receive blows than remain lonely and forgotten.

Some people masturbate because it is their only moment of pleasure. Alone, in bed, they can at last feel some pleasure.

In some hospitals or asylums, if the food is bad, or there is no work (or, if it exists, is tedious or badly paid), or the leisure activities indifferent, then people will experience a terrible boredom, a lack of life. To escape from this many will seek sexual pleasures alone or with others. There is nothing else for them to do; they seek pleasure where they can find it.

The tragedy is that sexuality outside a relationship, outside a true bond of friendship, is a terrible delusion. It is a pleasure which lasts only a fleeting moment, and after that moment there is nothing, no longer any relationship . . . nothing. One finds oneself alone, empty and in anguish.

In the past, masturbation was rigidly condemned. This condemnation led to fear, which nourished guilt and led to inhibitions, even hatred of oneself and one's body. Today, there is a tendency to say that masturbation is not serious, that we should let people do what they want, and that it is normal for an adolescent. It seems to me that the truth is between these two attitudes of rigidity and permissiveness. One must not condemn young people who masturbate. They have compulsions which they are not yet able to control or integrate. However, it is necessary to help them to stop. Masturbation can close them in on themselves and into a world of dreams and thus prevent them from entering into true relationships.

Pleasure is a very ambiguous reality. There are dangerous pleasures, deadly pleasures, and those which create a need, a habit (drugs, for example, not only imprison the person in habit but also within a world of imaginary excitement, and, at the same time, begin to destroy the brain). Such pleasures impede true spiritual growth. They keep one from knowing reality, from knowing one's true needs and the needs of others, from loving other people and from making an effort in the struggle for peace and justice. The pursuit of pleasure for oneself implies a certain indifference towards others; and, when the seeking becomes total, it cuts a person off from others completely. Beside the injustice created by those who oppress and torture the weak, there is also the injustice of those who are closed in on themselves, in their world of pleasure, refusing to share and communicate with others.

The pursuit of egotistical sexual pleasure can become like a drug, which prevents the heart from becoming sensitive to the needs and sufferings of others. It can enclose people within themselves, within their own feelings and subjective emotions, and cut them off from reality.

Pleasure, then, can be destructive, shutting a person up in a world of isolation and intensifying the anguish, an anguish which makes one seek other pleasures and compensations. It becomes a vicious circle. The need for drugs and alcohol becomes greater as the person craves for more and more pleasure, because the anguish and inner pain become greater. This search is endless and leads eventually to death: a human being is never satisfied and always wants more. This dependence which springs from anguish is not only a spiritual reality: the anguish takes flesh, in the body, in the blood, creating a physical dependence.

For the rich, there is always a danger of letting oneself be seduced by the attraction of instant pleasure which can be bought. In rich families, every material need and desire of the child can be immediately satisfied, and eventually the child becomes spoiled. The word 'spoiled' is significant.

There is, however, an education for hope which requires an inner strength. It involves the renunciation of certain immediate and superficial pleasures in order to realize deeper pleasures, those which open the person to higher and more universal realities in the world of art, of knowledge, of religion and of true relationships and service. For example, it takes an effort to restrain oneself in eating and drinking if one wants to give to those who are hungry.

THE DISCOVERY OF TRUE JOY

There are also those joys which open us to others and in some way strengthen us inwardly; they give us security and trust in ourselves, which in turn enable us to comprehend better the needs of others and to respond to them.

Such joys are a nourishment and a resource which relax us and, at the same time, give us energy to continue the struggle against all the forces of evil which tend to enclose us in the prison of egoism and fear. These joys will lead us along the way of love. When pleasure is taken as an end in itself, as an absolute, it closes the person in on him or herself. When it is taken as nourishment, it helps us to serve others better. Pleasure is then no longer a wall preventing us from seeing others; it becomes a 'go-between', just as parents are go-betweens, allowing the child to be integrated in the universe; without this intermediary, the little one is afraid, closes up in isolation, becomes aggressive. Through the presence of an intermediary, fear disappears and the child finds the confidence necessary to go towards others, to love them and to co-operate with them. So it is with pleasure in its most beautiful form.

The bonds of mutual attraction between a man and woman can be very fulfilling and authentic. With, and in, these bonds the man and woman can be intermediaries to one another, giving each other security, opening each other up to others and to the universe. But also, this attraction can close the man and woman in on themselves, and each one upon him or herself, hindering their harmonious and constructive integration into the universe.

One of the principal roles of education is to help someone to distinguish the pleasures which nourish and open one up from those pleasures which imprison, pleasures which bring true fulfil-ment from those which are only passing illusions. Education consists in more than simply forbidding false pleasures; rather, it helps the person to discover how they are false, or, at least, that there are others which bring a much deeper joy and, at the same time, give security, peace and confidence. The difficulty on the educational level is to know when to let a person discover by experience that certain pleasures are illusions and destructive, and when it is better simply to forbid the experience – hoping to prevent bad habits before they become rooted, but possibly arousing frustration and anger which can augment the desire. There are so many different situations, that it is impossible to lay down precise rules. The important thing is to try to discover which attitudes allow a person to grow most.

THE SEARCH FOR SEXUAL RELATIONS IN THE ABSENCE OF COMMUNITY AND CELEBRATION

It seems that in the culture of rich countries there is a link between the expression of genital sexuality and the disappearance of community life and the bonds of true friendship. The values of our society push people towards autonomy and individualism. To be strong is to have no need of another; to be free is to be dependent on no one. These are ideals which oppose that of community based on the acknowledgement of our gifts, our weaknesses, and our need of others. There is no longer, or at least very much less, a sense of sharing. Villages have lost their soul and a sense of celebration. In the big cities, no one knows anyone; each is isolated, barricaded within their own four walls. Large families, with all the uncles, aunts, grandparents, cousins, have disappeared. Even the nuclear family is in danger because there is no longer celebration together, no longer a sense of community. People find themselves isolated and anguished, often lacking inner strength. Therefore, they seek excitement in violent or erotic shows, drugs or alcohol. They throw themselves into the pursuit of political and other causes in a terrible hyperactivity, without sufficient reflection. Or they seek strong emotions in transitory, egotistical sexual relations without a deep intimacy of the heart and without covenant. In all these situations they risk losing themselves.

Forbidding genital sexuality outside marriage will not remedy the situation. What is needed is the creation of communities where people love each other deeply and where there is an authentic covenant relationship between them, a covenant which is celebrated with joy, enthusiasm and creativity. A world without joy and celebrations of this kind will necessarily engender superficial sexuality. When sexual relations between a man and a woman involve neither love nor celebration, when they are not the sign and fruit of a covenant, they cannot bring true joy. They are rather the fruit of anguish and come from the fear of isolation.

PEOPLE WITH MENTAL HANDICAPS HAVE A CAPACITY FOR
CELEBRATION

One of the things that strikes me most about those who have a mental handicap is their capacity for celebration. One might say that it is a special phenomenon of the communities of l'Arche (I speak of this in my book, *Community and Growth*). But, I notice this same phenomenon wherever there are people with a mental handicap. Many of them are not concerned about 'what others will think'. They love to fool around, to play and to laugh. At the heart of celebration, people with a mental handicap are so often ready to sing, clap their hands, even to dance, while people who are more rational and conventional are stiff, tense, unable to smile or even sing. At l'Arche, when we mime scenes from the Gospels, the assistants are always a little too self-conscious and nervous to play the part of Jesus. People with a mental handicap are more relaxed, freer and less concerned about what others think.

There is much enthusiasm in some countries for the 'normalization' of those with mental handicaps. This is excellent if, by normalization, we mean the exercise of the fundamental rights of all human beings: the right to have work, to use public transport and the public swimming pool, etc. But, it would be unjust not to respect the culture and the special needs of those who are mentally handicapped. They will never be intellectuals, so the vast majority will not be able to appreciate things that are intellectual and rational; they are much more intuitive and less verbal. Their culture and their own needs are more in the realm of affectivity. That is why they love celebrations in which they can actively participate.

Our modern culture no longer knows how to celebrate. It knows about 'parties' where one drinks, eats, laughs and meets others. It knows about leisure activities: television, shows, sport, dances, games, books, etc. It knows about holidays when one does what one wants; but it does not know what celebration is.

Celebration is a cry of joy and acknowledgement that our lives are woven together; it is the joyful recognition that we are bonded together with one another as part of the same body, that our differences represent a treasure and a richness, and that we can let down the barriers which keep us from one another. We rejoice at being able to share what is most profound and most vulnerable within us: we are bonded together in trust.

Celebration is a reality of community, springing from the union and communion between its members. Its purpose is not to prove anything. It is simply the pinnacle of community life, an expression of unity which, at the same time, forges a deeper unity.

Celebration involves the body and the senses; it involves music and song, coloured garments, flowers, beauty; it involves food and fun, movement and dance, joy and humour, prayer and thanksgiving. Each human reality has its place in celebration.

At l'Arche, the first thing we learned was how to celebrate birthdays: a moment to express, through the festivities, that someone is a special gift for the community; we talk of his or her life and special qualities. It is a time to say simply why we are happy the person is with us, helping us to build community. The person celebrated is the centre of the feast. We choose entertainment, presents and food according to his or her particular preferences, needs and sense of humour.

We also celebrate religious feasts, Christmas, Easter, and Pentecost – feasts which remind us how much God loves his people and how close he is to us. Humanity is not all alone among the suffering, inequalities and anguishes of our world. And the community is not alone either: God is watching over it and leading it. Each person is in the hands of the Father, no one is all alone.

We celebrate those who have been with l'Arche for ten years; we celebrate the end of the year by recalling all the events for which we give thanks. Every occasion is an opportunity for celebration.

When we celebrate we sing together, we laugh together, we pray together. This creates in the heart of each one a sense of belonging to the group, and to the community. We are made to be together, to live and work together, each one in his or her place. Among us there are bonds created by God; there is a covenant. And that covenant is not something which stifles personal growth or hinders it. On the contrary, it confirms our growth and calls us to go further: it liberates. It is God who called us from our isolation in order to live together; it is he who has chosen us and brought us to l'Arche to build community. He has given each one of us a gift which we must use and develop so that the construction will be beautiful.

Each group of men and women have their celebrations with its symbols, its language, its costumes which unify the members and give them a sense of belonging. Armed forces have parades (but this is not celebration!); African villages have their dances, their rituals and their ceremonies of initiation; clubs have their traditions and their 'liturgies'; psychoanalysts of different schools have their language and their symbols.

Depending on the structures and kinds of groupings,

celebrations can close the members in on themselves or open them to others and to God. The sense of belonging and of fellowship can be exclusive or it can be open. Exclusiveness implies elitism; it is then a show of power: we are the best, the strongest, the saved, the predestined. This is not true celebration. Openness implies humility and a certain poverty: no one is excluded. At the heart of the celebration is the presence of the weakest and the poorest people. A true celebration is one open to all those who recognize and wish to live the covenant, to celebrate it and give thanks.

At the heart of the Christian community is the celebration of the Eucharist. At the heart of this feast it is God who has become small and poor, hidden under the appearances of bread and wine. He comes to give himself to the little ones and to the poorest. The Eucharist is the celebration of the love of Jesus and of his resurrection. It announces his return; it is a sign of hope. But the Eucharist is also the presence of suffering. It is the supreme sacrifice of Jesus, where he gave his life; his blood is spilt, his body given. All the miseries and sufferings of humanity, all the brokenness, is present there. It is the sign of the fecundity of all suffering offered in union with Jesus, whose suffering saves and liberates.

The Eucharist is, *par excellence*, a celebration of unity, giving a sense of belonging to Jesus and to his body which is the Church, and to that cell of the Church which is our particular community. What is special in the Eucharist is that it is both a community celebration and a very intimate, personal reality. The Eucharist begins with the Word, community song and prayer; it ends in silence, a heart-to-heart relationship with Jesus, where each one eats his body and drinks his blood. It is a moment of communion: 'He who eats my body and drinks my blood lives in me and I in him.' The two become one in one flesh, the flesh of Christ. Other celebrations can give a sense of belonging but they do not always end in intimacy. They are not necessarily an experience of personal friendship with another. This is lived at other moments.

The Eucharist is the reminder that community is not an easy place, but a place of growth in the heart of God. The Eucharist is a nourishment to help us walk along the road of love and liberation. It binds together, in a mysterious way, the pain and the joys of community, the covenant, a word of hope, an intimate communion with God and with one's brothers and sisters.

A community which no longer celebrates its joy at being together, united to God, and open to others is a dying community. It is made up only of rules and regulations, perhaps even of promises and vows. But it has lost its soul; it is only a skeleton. The heart of a community shows itself through the different forms of celebration and in the love, the mutual trust, the joy of being together, brothers and sisters, working towards the same goal.

CELEBRATION, AGGRESSION AND FORGIVENESS

One of the functions of celebration is to liberate aggression, which is like a wall separating people. Aggression can be offensive and defensive. It protects and repulses. It hides that which is most profound and most intimate in us, the vulnerability of our hearts, our longing to love and to be loved, our thirst for tenderness, for compassion and understanding, and for personal relationships. This aggression or hardness is the result of wounds, misunderstandings, injustices, and incomprehension, of guilt and of fear. Aggression divides; it is partisan; it creates blocks; it closes people inside themselves; it separates; it causes tension. If it takes root, it destroys community.

There is a visible aggression which can be dangerous when it leads to division, to schism, and tears the community apart. But visible aggression can lead to dialogue and to forgiveness, which allows growth in truth and the discovery of a new unity. In effect, there is a healthy aggression which is a cry for space, a cry for truth, a cry for recognition.

There is also a hidden, sly aggression which is never expressed. People are too afraid of the manifestations of aggression, and of the diversities and the splits at the centre of the community. So, the members hide themselves from each other, speaking only of superficialities. There is no true dialogue; subjects which risk bringing the discord to the surface are taboo. Conversation conforms to the rules of politeness, but the fear and the lack of trust in each other remains; there are impenetrable barriers between people. The aggression is there, undermining all true relationship, but everybody pretends that all is well and that there is unity. In order to arrive at a true unity, we have to acknowledge consciously the division, the aggression, the fear which lives in our hearts; only then will we find the remedies and be able to come to dialogue and forgiveness.

There is a link between forgiveness and celebration. Celebration implies forgiveness and flows from it. When the prodigal son returned home after a debauched life, the father forgave him and gathered everyone together for a feast. He said to his servants: 'Hurry up! Bring the most beautiful robe and put it on him, Place a ring on his finger and shoes on his feet. Bring the fatted calf, kill it, we will eat and celebrate because my son who was dead has returned to life. He was lost and he is found! Let us celebrate!'[1]

Some people would like community celebrations to be spontaneous; they say they can celebrate only if they feel like it. But if we waited until everyone spontaneously feels like it, there would not be very many celebrations! Between a very rigid ritual and a spontaneous manifestation, there is a middle road. Celebrations must be well prepared. It is important to plan the songs, and the order of the various activities, but at the same time remaining flexible and able to change: to prolong certain moments of grace and times of silence, or to cut things short if necessary. Often it is the unexpected and the spontaneous which nourishes most. But this spontaneity, which comes from the presence of the Holy Spirit in people, only makes sense if it springs from within a well planned celebration.

Many of those with a mental handicap need to be stimulated and called into activities. This demands energy. It would be so much easier to put them in front of the television, or a show that others perform, or simply let them do their own thing. But once they are called to the celebration, they become the heart of it, and draw others into it, creating a warmth and special joy.

THE CELEBRATION OF UNITY

The joy which flows from the physical union of intimacy, when it is true, is the joy of love, the joy of knowing that one is not alone on the road of our earthly pilgrimage. Physical intimacy

1. Luke 15:22–4.

is the summit of a friendship which also implies daily companionship. The joy of the wedding feast is the joy of unity. The book of Genesis and the Gospel speak of man and woman called to become one flesh. The word, 'flesh', as used here, does not simply signify a physical reality or, still less, that flesh is opposed to spirit. It means the profound unity of two persons, who become a sign of the presence of the Holy Trinity. In another context, Jesus prayed that his disciples might be one as the Father and he are one (see John, chapter 17). It is impossible not to connect the two texts, especially since St Paul, in his epistle to the Ephesians, compares the union of the Church with Jesus Christ to the union between man and woman in love.

When the two spouses give themselves to each other in complete trust, in total gift, and in great tenderness, it is a celebration of unity. It is not simply a celebration of the love between the spouses, but also of the unity between the parents and their children. It puts the official seal on the unity of the family and its vocation to service.

John Paul II commented on the text from Genesis (2:23–5) where man meets woman for the first time, 'This at last is bone of my bones and flesh of my flesh. She shall be called Woman because she is taken out of Man.' The text continues: 'Therefore, a man leaves his father and his mother and cleaves to his wife, and they become one flesh. And the man and his wife were both naked and were not ashamed.' Pope John Paul II says that this text announces the first celebration of humanity with an experience of the spiritual significance of the body.[2]

According to psychologists, the great search made by human beings is the search for unity: unity with God, unity with the cosmos, unity with each other. They say that the deepest cry of the unconscious is to find our lost unity. Before birth, the infant is not conscious of the unity it has with its mother or the way in which his or her personality is being formed by this unity (or sometimes by the lack of it). But, from the time the baby leaves the security, the peace and the harmony of its mother's womb, it is in search of another unity . . . The union of spouses is one of the major experiences of that search for the lost unity, but it is attained only if the two persons consciously give themselves one to the other.

2. General audience of 20 February 1980.

The unity which is celebrated by the two spouses is not, first of all, a material unity, the union of their bodies. It is born from the fact that they are one heart, one soul, one spirit. Man and woman, profoundly different in some aspects, are companions for life, special friends united in tenderness, in their vision of the world and in their love of God. The spousal union is a profound unity, a sign of other unities. But it is not the only one; there are others. If those who cannot marry, or are not called to marry, do not find ways to celebrate unity in other forms, their hearts and their bodies will cry out; the physical and biological need of sexuality will cry out and seek ways of fulfilment other than in true covenant.

This is why celebrations at l'Arche have a very deep meaning. If a home or community forgets these celebrations, in all probability, there will be a tendency to sexual immaturity among its members. Community celebrations must always be celebrations of unity, celebrations of a covenant.

HAPPINESS

The human being thirsts for happiness. Those who have the impression that they will never be happy enter into the process of death. They find themselves alone, faced with their limits, and their poverty; they succumb to sadness and despair. Despair is life which turns in against itself. When life does not flow outwards and bear fruit, it will destroy itself.

Throughout the ages, one of the great symbols of the happiness sought by each human being is that of the wedding feast. This symbol of unity is so powerful that the mass media uses it in order to sell all kinds of products: in order to be loved, to find a partner, you must wear such and such a garment, use such and such a perfume, be seen eating such and such a cheese! This symbol is also the *leitmotiv* for art, for films, and for songs. Humanity is always searching for that unchanging love which will take away all pain, all suffering, all division, all war.

Marxism hopes to establish a perfect socialistic state where, after and beyond all the struggles and warfare, everyone will live in continual celebration, where all will celebrate equality since there will be only one class, one people; the proletariat having conquered the bourgeoisie.

The final goal of mankind, to which we all aspire, is that unity where there will be no more struggle and warfare. Struggle, in effect, implies the possibility of being vanquished and oppressed, and thus to be isolated. The wedding feast is the final goal of all struggle since it is the celebration of love.

But this quest for unity is even more deeply rooted in humanity. It is inscribed in all the great religions and, in particular, in Hinduism and Buddhism. It is found in the Judeo-Christian tradition, where it is said that at the end there will be one people, one nation, one city, the heavenly Jerusalem, where there will be no more war. In the effort to express the unity of this people of God, Scripture uses the symbols of the wedding feast. In Revelation, John sees a new heaven and a new earth:

I saw the holy city, and the new Jerusalem, coming down from God out of heaven, as beautiful as a bride all dressed for her husband. Then I heard a loud voice call from the throne, 'You see this city. Here God lives among men. He will make his home among them; they shall be his people, and he will be their God; his name is God-with-them. He will wipe away all tears from their eyes; there will be no more death, and no more mourning or sadness. The world of the past has gone.' (Revelation 21:1–4)

The Kingdom of God is like a celebration of love, 'a wedding feast' (Matthew 22:1–10), a celebration of unity.

Those with mental handicaps, like all human beings, yearn for this celebration of unity. It is their deepest yearning. And that celebration of love is something which flows from the whole being.

But how can this unity of love be celebrated? That is the fundamental question for all of us. In order to celebrate this unity, we must be liberated from our egoism and hardness, and go beyond ourselves, opening up to others. If we remain imprisoned in the search to satisfy our own needs, we can only celebrate our own acquisitions and possessions; we cannot celebrate love and unity.

To celebrate unity is to discover the unity that people have among themselves. St Paul compares the Church to a body in which each person, with his own gifts, is a member.[3] Human

3. 1 Corinthians 12.

beings, united by Christ, become a single body, a single spirit. No longer are they rivals, living in competition. No longer do they see differences as a threat, but as a treasure. They live in harmony with each other; they no longer need to attack each other but, on the contrary, they need each other with their different gifts. When we discover the riches of interdependence, we are no longer alone; we are together, helping one another, each one with his or her differences and gifts. Only then can that which is most profound in each one be awakened: the vulnerable heart, often hidden behind walls of aggression and defence, but capable of welcoming God and others without losing what is most precious in self, one's liberty, one's deepest identity, one's love.

There is nothing more beautiful on earth than people who have trust in each other. The work of God is all that fosters the growth of trust. The work of the evil spirit is all that separates: breakdown of relationship between people, lack of trust, and doubt.

The celebration of unity is celebration of the trust we have in each other. Yet, our hearts remain wounded. In each of us is sin and evil; we are not yet in heaven. Celebrations on earth are essentially celebrations of hope. But that hope does not deceive, because it is founded on our trust in Jesus Christ, who has conquered death and evil. It is he who calls us to live a covenant with him and asks us to invite others to live it with us.

Conclusion

Community is a place where people grow towards wholeness. Through authentic relationships which touch and call forth each one in their most intimate self, through a sense of belonging, through a real fruitfulness at personal and communal levels, through celebrations and, above all, through a life in communion with Jesus, each one can gradually move toward the integration of his sexual instincts. But this community life implies that each one says, anew each day, 'Yes' to one's own growth. If community is a place of beneficial relationships, it is also a place of struggle and inner pain. When we live alone, it is easy to believe we are holy; when we live with others we see that we are not. We discover quickly, in the depths of ourselves, areas of hate and anguish, of jealousy and fear, of blockages and the need to dominate or to prove one's worth.

Human life never remains static. It is either deepening and continually opening towards reality and truth, or closing up and regressing into itself. A human being either opens him or herself more and more in liberty and trust or closes in on him or herself behind barriers of fear. A community can only be a place of healing and growth if it remains dynamic in love and hope. We know that communities can become soulless institutions, administrations, 'hierarchies', places where the rule and organization are more important than communion and friendship among its members. A community needs to be constantly nourished and revitalized, otherwise it risks closing in on itself. Then it is no longer a community.

The challenge of l'Arche is precisely that. Each of our communities has experienced the forces of despair which spring from inside or outside the community and which stifle life; each has experienced also the forces of hope which give life. To live in community is a struggle against the forces of despair.

However, there are certain laws which must be known and respected: we must continually bring to the consciousness of people, in a dynamic way, the goals and objectives of the community in order to stimulate the motivations and energies of each one; we must have constant recourse to prayer, putting ourselves humbly before God; we must recognize the necessity of true and simple dialogue between each other, and listen to each one, particularly to those in a minority and the most poor; we must learn to forgive and to celebrate while remaining poor, because riches, like comfort, smother energies; we must have recourse to the wisdom of experienced men and women who come from outside to help evaluate the community. If we are not attentive to these things, we will gradually lose the inspiration that carries us forward. And if we lose that we will begin to build barriers around ourselves; we will move towards division, separation, divorce and brokenness, towards the death of the community.

When a community becomes lukewarm and mediocre, its members suffer all kinds of frustrations. Relationships are no longer warm and authentic. Energy to welcome, to love, and to celebrate is drained away; a sense of sterility dominates the group. When there is no longer an outlet for the emotions of each one, at a deep level, then aggression, sexual deviations and blockages appear.

Laws, rules and regulations cannot solve problems that arise. They tend only to aggravate things. They increase frustration, guilt and inner tensions, which must finally seek relief in some kind of compensation.

Permissiveness with regard to erotic sexuality, cut off from covenant relationships, is the fruit of a culture without hope. The true solution lies, not in condemning this frenetic sexuality, but in the rediscovery of hope. In our times, the family community tends to be easily broken, with all the disastrous consequences this brings to the children, giving rise to anguished individualism, and frequently extreme fragility. It seems to me that we cannot recover health in human relationships, and the necessary energies to create communities which permit the integration of sexual drives, unless we turn to the Gospel and the hope which it gives us. Ethics alone is not sufficient, because knowledge of a law does not give the necessary energy to abide by it.

It is especially difficult for those with a mental handicap to find a harmony in their lives if they are not in a true community. They have such need of relationships, intimacy, fecundity and celebration. It is not surprising that some turn to sexual relations, hoping against hope that they will find peace in this. But many are disappointed by these superficial relationships which do not lead to a true and permanent friendship, to a real covenant and sense of belonging one to another. Some, however, find a balance, albeit precarious, in the life of the couple where there is a friendship. I feel it is more just and more true to guide such couples towards marriage rather than leave them on a plateau of doubt concerning the permanence of their relationship. Instead of accepting too quickly that couples are made and unmade, it is better to call them either to be really faithful to the relationship (and to give them the help they need for that) or to a dynamic community life.

I am moved by the sufferings of so many parents who are obliged to put their children in centres which encourage sexual activity as a liberation, and which lack a vision of faith that would give the unifying and inspirational force necessary for true community life. We have let parents manage as best they could alone. It is not surprising that parents coming from different philosophical and religious backgrounds have come together to create schools and residences, though, because of their very diversity, they have often not been able to create true communities, with the faith and inspiration that that implies.

Perhaps it is not too late to reverse the trend, if men and women of faith, open to the reality of community and conscious of the value of those with a mental handicap and their importance in society, work together to create or regenerate communities. Then perhaps there could be a rediscovery of the values of welcome and of love, right at the heart of society, where those with a handicap will be able to find their proper place and make their own contribution.

But, as long as there are no real communities, those with a mental handicap will find themselves at the bottom of the ladder of society, isolated, in anguish and in despair.

I am concerned about the future for people with mental handicaps. Today, when everything is professionalized and considered from an economic viewpoint, the great risk is that those with a mental handicap will be done away with, because they cost too much. Certainly, efforts will be made to educate those who are less handicapped, for 'normal' work or for work in sheltered workshops; but those who are more handicapped are in danger of being eliminated. Already, prenatal diagnosis, which in itself could be a good thing if there were remedies, leads quite frequently to abortion. And, it is well known that more and more babies born with a handicap are being killed at birth.

People with mental handicaps are an enigma for our society. Their very presence brings up many questions which are more or less unanswerable. It is difficult to see the meaning of their existence. Unable to develop their will and reason, their lives often appear fruitless and futile. In today's society, which is so organized and structured, they are seen as an economic burden. Their presence disturbs people.

Very often people look upon l'Arche as if we are completely mad; I realize this more and more. We consider those whom society devalues as valuable, and capable of awakening what is most precious in a human being – the heart, generosity, the dynamism of love. They incite us to put our intelligence at the service of love. They have a capacity to heal others by calling them to unify within themselves their deep emotions, their capacity for love and their reason. Thus, they can become sources of life.

A society which discards those who are non-productive and weak, risks an exaggerated development of reason, organization, aggression and the desire to dominate. It becomes a society without a heart, without kindness – a rational and sad society, lacking celebration, divided within itself and given to competition, rivalry and, finally, violence.

The Gospel alone reveals to us the true meaning of the poor, the weak, and the non-productive. The message of Jesus is clear: the Good News is announced to the poor. And that good news is that they will never be abandoned; they are loved by the Father who takes care of them. They *do* have a place; they *do* have value. Hidden in them is a mystery. In drawing near to them through the heart, we draw near to God. Thus, they reveal what is most precious in each person: the capacity to love. They have a mysterious power that enables people to open up to each other.

However, they can also reveal that which is hardest, most egotistical and most intolerant in a human being, precisely

172

because they disturb and challenge people. They probe those places of fear, hate and anguish which are in each of us. Their cry for friendship reveals to us the fear that we have of love and, thus, they can stir up hate. The rich fear the poor, who disturb them! That is why they arrange things in such a way that they never see them or have contact with them. And then, they try to justify this brutal rejection. But the revelation of the presence of fear and hate in each of us can be salutary; it shows us the truth of our being, that truth which we do not like to acknowledge. No human being likes to have pointed out the powers of evil and death which are in him or her. We always want to appear good and perfect; we want to believe ourselves just; we do not want others to know that we can be wrong and that there is evil in us. But healing cannot take place until our illusions have been exposed and we acknowledge our human reality. I must admit that it was only when I had touched my own misery and the hatred within me that I was able to be touched by the mercy of God and discover the mystery of Jesus, gentle healer of hearts and saviour of our brokenness. It was only then that I was able myself to touch, with a compassionate heart, the misery of others without crushing them.

It is true that the poor heal the hearts of the rich. They lead them to discover their own poverty. The rich, in the biblical sense of the word, have everything except the essential: the capacity to give, and to give of themselves. The words of Jesus need not surprise us: 'How hard it is for those who have riches to enter the kingdom of God! It is easier for a camel to pass through the eye of a needle . . .' The poor help the rich to discover the value of love and sharing.

Carl Jung once said at a conference[1] how much he admired Christians because they saw Christ in the poor in those who are hungry, naked, in hospital and in prison, and in those who are strangers. But what he could not understand was that they could not see Christ in their own poverty. We are all running away from the consciousness of our own misery. We prefer to live in the illusions of our perfection. In order to face the reality of our limits and our poverty, is it not essential that first of all we become aware that we are beloved by God *in* this very poverty? More and more, I sense that only this acknowledgement of

1. To Protestant pastors at Strasbourg, May 1932. *Collected Works*, vol. XI.

our wounds and our poverty will enable us to live a true friendship with those having a mental handicap. Often we believe ourselves superior to them, their 'benefactors' and 'educators', and so we are unable to create community with them. The acknowledgement of our own limits and wounds will allow us, in truth, to draw near to their limits and wounds. Friendship begins with the acceptance of others as they are, without first wanting to change them. It is this friendship that the person with a mental handicap needs in order to leave the prison of loneliness and begin to live.

The danger of our civilization is the race to climb the ladder of success, of power, and of possession. This also encourages isolation, as we rise to the top we are more and more lonely; it creates a division between those who achieve success and those who do not and who then become discouraged and aggressive. Should we not reverse the race and rather encourage people to descend the ladder in order to meet those who are poorest and create relationship with them? We will then create what everyone most needs: a true community. Then, all together, with the most poor at the heart of that community, we will celebrate our covenant. But who has the authority, and above all, the necessary credibility to reverse the course of history? Is it not up to each one of us?

We all have to choose between two ways of being crazy: the foolishness of the Gospel and the non-sense of the values of our world. The Gospel is crazy: it sees in the poor a sign and a sacrament of God, thus revealing the mystery of Jesus and leading us to a true inner freedom, through a community life with celebrations and relationships. The values of the world are mad: they lead human beings to seek riches for themselves, which cause them to scorn and reject others and to build protective walls around themselves, and finally to arm themselves for better defence. And this leads finally to destruction. John Halsey, an Anglican priest of the Community of the Transfiguration in Scotland near Edinburgh, once told us: 'Either we will continue to walk *on* the poor and that will lead to the explosion of nuclear arms; or we will walk *with* the poor and that will lead to the transfiguration in Jesus Christ.'

Those with a mental handicap will be able to live humanly only if they find their place in authentic community life. But that community life is not possible without the inspiration of the

174

Gospel which sees the poorest people as a positive source of inspiration and authority as service and not privilege.

Indeed, such a community life is necessary for all men and women on our earth. I doubt whether it is possible to resist the seductions of riches or of power and all the superficial pleasures that are offered to distract us, if we do not share in a community of forgiveness and celebration, centred on the poor.

The more I experience my own humanity and that of others, the more I am aware of the depth of the wound which lives in the heart of each human being, whether it is husbands who hide or take refuge in work because they feel guilty and are no longer attracted to their wives, or wives who are bitter and wounded by lack of attention and love from their husbands, or parents in conflict with their children, or children stifled by parents who are too possessive: all are wounded. We are wounded by sickness, wounded by a handicap, wounded by the death of a dear one, wounded by the past, and by the non-acceptance of ourselves. We are wounded by failures in work, and especially by failures in our relationships. We are wounded by hate and fear, by the inability to forgive and the experience of rejection which makes us in turn reject, and by the blockages between people and groups. We are wounded by our own unfaithfulness and sin. Psychology may help unravel the origins of some of these wounds, in the acknowledgement of which we may be helped to touch with less fear the pain that has been hidden in our depths. But it cannot heal the wounded heart or fill its terrible emptiness or wipe out the guilt of having wounded others.

We are in a world where these wounds continually fester. Fidelity no longer has any value; sometimes it is even ridiculed. We are more preoccupied with the acquisition of riches and success. Above all, we seek to avoid the pain in our hearts by compensations and distractions which can never truly satisfy. Today there is a serious crisis for families: more and more marriages fail, bringing a deep guilt in the heart of the man and the woman and suffering for the children. These children will lack emotional maturity and stability; many retain a deep insecurity or fear, leading perhaps to aggression. As they grow older many will have difficulty integrating their sexuality; their anguish and their need to be loved will push them too quickly towards 'a love' without love.

The men and women of our society are emotionally vulnerable

and fragile because they lack the love of a family or a community or, in other words, a milieu which gives support, security, strength, peace and relaxation.

As authentic communities are born, hearts are slowly being healed, but the acquisition of maturity can take a long time and a certain vulnerability always remains. This vulnerability is the lot of humanity. It comes from a dissonance between the desire in the heart of each one of us to be happy and the realities of life. Each one of us experiences frustrations and dissatisfactions. Our hearts suffer from loneliness, and feelings of failure and guilt; lacking confidence in ourselves we are afraid.

But, if we live in a community, especially one anchored in Jesus, we find hope and strength to live the daily life, to struggle, despite all the forces of opposition, for a world of greater justice and brotherly love. We find there hope in the face of the anguish and the conflicts of our world: a hope which comes from the heart of God teaching us how to love, to understand, to forgive and to build peace.

L'Arche is only beginning. Little by little, we discover what we are called to be. We do not have all the answers to the sufferings of members of the community. Certainly there are men and women who have grown toward an inner freedom, but there are also those who manifest violence, depression, sexual deviations and emotional blockages, others are more or less imprisoned in anger and psychoses. But, isn't this the lot of so many other men and women in our world? Our role is to become their friends, to help them to carry their sufferings and to find a little light which will allow them to advance. In trying to revive that tiny flame, so fragile and precious, in the heart of the most poor, l'Arche wants to become a little sign of hope in our anguished world.

The mystery of those with a mental handicap – and we could say the same thing for all weak and rejected people – is that they are a source of life and truth, if we welcome them, enter into communion with them and put ourselves at their service.

In being welcomed, they find life and hope; but, in addition, they give life and hope. In our world, with its divisions and hardness, often full of hate and strife they teach men and women the way to trust, to simplicity, to love and to unity.

This book is a witness to what we have experienced and discovered in living close to those who have a mental handicap.

Their cry for relationship, for authentic love and for fruitfulness – far more profound than their desire for sexual pleasure – has revealed to us the cry of all human beings for relationship, for authentic love, and for fruitfulness. We have so much to learn from those who, though stripped of power and knowledge, are so rich in their hearts and in their simplicity.